KU-207-986

ned halley's
★★★★★★★★★

super
market
wine

REPORT

foulsham
LONDON • NEW YORK • TORONTO • SYDNEY

foulsham

The Publishing House, Bennetts Close, Cippenham,
Slough, Berkshire, SL1 5AP, England

ISBN 0-572-02943-8

Copyright © 2004 Ned Halley

Series, format and layout design © 2004 W. Foulsham & Co. Ltd

Printed in Great Britain by St. Edmundsbury Press, Bury St. Edmunds

Contents

——A Personal Word——

This is an exclusive guide. It describes the wines on sale only in that clique of retailers formed by the larger supermarket chains. It is in these places that we buy three-quarters of all the wine we drink at home.

Each of the big chains sells several hundred different wines, and it is by no means easy to guess what an untried bottle might taste like or whether it will turn out to be good value for money. The point of this book is to give the reader some clues.

To make it as straightforward as possible, I have divided the thing up according to the supermarkets themselves. Under each name, I have arranged the recommended wines first by colour, second by price range, finally by country of origin – because that's the way the supermarkets arrange the wines on their shelves.

With very few exceptions, all the wines mentioned here are recommendations. I have a simple scoring system up to 10 points to indicate quality-value ratio (see Scoring System on page 24) and anything scoring 7 or above is, I believe, worth buying at the price shown.

This is an exclusive guide in another sense. It leaves out the very well known brands that are available in most, if not all, supermarkets. This does not mean I do not recommend Jacob's Creek, Ernest & Julio Gallo, Blossom Hill and so forth. It just means that I am not willing to fill the following pages with their eternally repeating names.

The wines that do get mentioned are in the main less well known. Many are the own-brands of the supermarkets in question. As many as I can find are from quirky individual growers who make wine in small quantities.

Admittedly, supermarkets are not famous for stocking wines produced on a very small scale. When you have 600 branches to supply and expectations of shifting every wine in large, fast volume, a couple of hundred cases of some rare vintage are not going to go very far. But some supermarkets do nevertheless include such wines among their faster-moving stock, and they are well worth seeking out.

Most of the wines in this book are in the price categories that account for most sales. About 88 per cent of wines sold for drinking at home cost under £5. About 18 per cent fall into the £4.50 to £6 bracket and a mere 4 per cent cost above £6.

Naturally, I believe most of the best wines are accounted for in that exclusive 4 per cent, and there are a good few of them in these pages. But the real point of this book is to recommend wines at prices that I – and you – know we're willing to pay.

The good news is that there is a lot of wine out there at affordable prices. Britain has the best choice of wine of any country in the world, and despite the monstrous taxation levied on it, it seems to me to be a luxury we can all afford – and a thoroughly healthy and civilising luxury at that.

I must apologise in advance for the inevitable fact that some of the wines I have recommended will have been discontinued or replaced with a new vintage or increased (they're never decreased) in price by the time you are reading this.

And I must reiterate the plea that what I say about the wines and the retailers is based on my personal knowledge or understanding. Taste in all things is personal, and more so than most when it comes to wine. But I hope the impressions I have given of the hundreds of wines recommended in this guide will tempt you to try some new styles and flavours, and to look beyond all those beckoning brand names to the genuine, individual wines still clinging to their shelf space.

Introduction

The supermarkets have the take-home market for wine just about completely sewn up. Nearly eight bottles out of every ten are bought from multiples and the traditional off-licence shops are having a relatively hard time of it.

I say relatively, because the wine business is booming and this means all kinds of retailers can benefit from the growth in wine drinking if they are any good. Sales of wine have increased by 6 per cent in terms of value in the last year and are predicted to continue to grow at this sort of rate for years to come.

As the overall market expands, so does the top end. Nine out of ten bottles bought still cost under £5, but the proportion of wines costing between £4.50 and £6.00 is moving up. Last year saw a modest rise from 16 to 18 per cent of the total, but this is nevertheless an encouraging sign for a business that is forever anxious to see its customers trade up a bit.

And wine prices in Britain are moving up anyway. This is due partly to the slide of sterling against the euro – something like 15 per cent over the year – but there has also been a contribution from the Chancellor of the Exchequer. Mr Brown's 2003 Budget might have been written off by the pundits as a non-event, but it has unquestionably had an interesting impact on wine prices. The Chancellor added about 4p per bottle to the excise duty on table wine, taking it to about £1.19 – further endangering that already rare species, the £2.99 bottle of supermarket wine.

This is how the price is arrived at: the supermarket pays the supplier 80p for the bottled wine, 30p of which the supplier spent on shipping it to the UK. The supermarket then pays the excise duty, which takes the price paid to £2.00.

Now the supermarket adds the standard 30 per cent mark-up, so the value becomes £2.60. Finally, VAT is added to this total, taking the on-shelf price to £3.05. Result: if supermarkets and wine merchants want to continue to sell wine at under £3 they are going to have to persuade producers to take less than 50p a bottle for it.

Some producers, clearly, are not going to swallow this, and so supermarkets are now full of wines that used to conform to 'price points' of £2.99 etc., but which have been upped to odd-looking tags of £3.03, £4.03 – even to £9.03 and £11.03. It looks as if the supermarkets just can't or won't keep on absorbing the extra duty.

I have noticed, though, that most of the wines with these odd new price tags are from within the European Union. New World wine prices look more static, and this must be because sterling has done a lot better against the US and Australian dollars, the wretched South African rand and the wobbly currencies of South America than it has against the euro.

This hardly bodes well for Old World wine producers, of course, and can only contribute to the astounding trends of the last couple of years, in which Australia has overtaken France as our principal supplier. The current picture is that three-quarters of all the wine we drink in Britain comes from just five nations. It goes like this, in terms of the money we spend:

Australia	23.4%
France	21.3%
Italy	10.4%
USA	10.0%
South Africa	9.1%

The rest is shared by nations you might have expected would be bigger suppliers than the US and South Africa – namely Spain and Portugal, Argentina and Chile, plus Germany, Bulgaria, Hungary and New Zealand.

But everyone wants a piece of the action, because Britain is the world's biggest importer of quality wines, and getting bigger every day. Headlines such as 'Wine is the new beer' are commonplace and sales in the last year rose in the 'off trade' – wine to drink at home – to 830 million bottles. Add the 198 million bottles we drank 'on trade' in pubs, bars and restaurants (a 10 per cent increase on the previous year) and we can be seen to be turning into a nation of wine drinkers.

And we are even more so than the official figures suggest. The Wine and Spirit Association estimates that for every six bottles of wine we buy in Britain, we drink an extra bottle 'personally imported' from France. This is legitimate wine, bought at the French duty rate of 2p a bottle instead of the UK's £1.19.

So we drink about 1.2 billion bottles of wine a year – 20 bottles per head of population or, more relevantly, 40 bottles per head of the wine-drinking population (two-thirds of all adults, apparently). It sounds a lot, but it's still less per capita than other northern European countries such as the Netherlands and Denmark, and less than half the consumption in wine-producing countries including Italy and Portugal.

We have, in other words, a long way to go in terms of quantity. I hope, too, that we have a similar distance to travel in terms of quality and choice. As the British market 'matures' and more of us seek to trade up to more interesting wines, I sincerely hope the supermarkets will be there, expanding their ranges to tempt us.

The Choice

This book categorises the wines by nation of origin. This is largely to follow the manner in which retailers arrange their wines, but also because it is the country or region of origin that still most distinguishes one style of wine from another. True, wines are now commonly labelled most prominently with their constituent grape variety, but to classify all the world's wines into the small number of principal grape varieties would make for categories of an unwieldy size.

Chardonnay and Sauvignon Blanc are overwhelmingly dominant among whites, and four grapes, Cabernet Sauvignon, Merlot, Shiraz and Tempranillo, account for a very high proportion of red wines made worldwide.

But each area of production still – in spite of creeping globalisation – puts its own mark on its wines. Chardonnays from France remain (for the moment at least) quite distinct from those of Australia. Cabernet Sauvignon grown in a cool climate such as that of Bordeaux is a very different wine from Cabernet cultivated in the cauldron of the Barossa.

Of course there are 'styles' that winemakers worldwide seek to follow. Yellow, oaky Chardonnays of the type pioneered in South Australia are now made in South Africa, too – and in new, high-tech wineries in New Zealand and Chile, Spain and Italy. But the variety is still wide. Even though the 'upfront' high-alcohol wines of the New World have grabbed so much of the market, France continues to make the elegant wines it has always made in its classic regions. Germany still produces racy, delicate Rieslings, and the distinctive zones of Italy, Portugal and Spain make ever-more characterful wines from indigenous grapes (as opposed to imported global varieties).

Among less expensive wines, the theme is, admittedly, very much a varietal one. The main selling point for most 'everyday' wines is the grape of origin rather than the country of origin. It makes sense, because the characteristics of various grape varieties do a great deal to identify taste. A bottle of white wine labelled 'Chardonnay' can reasonably be counted on to deliver that distinctive peachy or pineappley smell and soft, unctuous apple flavours. A Sauvignon Blanc should evoke gooseberries, green fruit and grassy freshness. And so on.

For all the domination of Chardonnay and Cabernet, there are plenty of other grape varieties making their presence felt. Argentina, for example, has revived the fortunes of several French and Italian varieties that had become near-extinct at home. And the grape that (in my view) can make the most exciting of white wines, the Riesling, is now doing great things in the southern hemisphere as well as at home in Germany.

The global varieties are, indeed, everywhere, but this book describes wines made from no fewer than 60 different grape varieties (see Glossary starting on page 131), grown in every corner of the wine making world. Let's hope this generous and growing choice is the shape of things to come.

The Price

How do retailers price their wines? Some bottles do seem inexplicably cheap, others unjustifiably expensive. But there is often a simple explanation. Big retailers work to price points. In wine, these are £2.99, £3.49, £3.99, even £9.99. You'll find very few bottles priced anywhere between these 50p spacings. A wine that wouldn't be profitable at £4.99 but would be at, say, £5.11, is priced at £5.49 in the hope that shoppers won't be wise to the fact that it is relatively poor value.

It's true that there are some wines on supermarket shelves priced at £3.29, £3.79 etc. And 2003 has seen, for the first time I can remember, some supermarkets pass the Budget's 4p rise in excise duty directly on to the customer, creating a new kind of price ending in 0.3 pence. But the .99 price point is still dominant, and I suspect will continue to be so for a very long time to come.

Price can be a poor guide to quality even at the best of times. The only means by which any of us can determine a wine's value is on personal taste. The ideal bottle is one you like very much and would buy again at the same price without demur.

But just for curiosity's sake, it's fun to know what the wine itself actually costs, and what the retailer is making on it. The table overleaf shows how the costs break down in a French wine costing £4.49 at a supermarket. This is a slightly unusual purchase by a supermarket, because the wine is being bought direct from the vineyard where it was made. Usually, retail multiples buy their wines by a less-strenuous method, from agents and distributors in the UK.

Price paid by supermarket to supplier in France for the bottled wine	£1.40
Transport and insurance to UK	£0.28
Excise duty	£1.19
Cost to supermarket	£2.87
Supermarket's routine mark-up at 30%	£0.86
VAT at 17.5% on marked-up price	£0.65
Provisional shelf price	£4.38
Adjustment in price/VAT to price point	£0.11
Shelf price in supermarket	£4.49

The largest share of the money appears to go to the producer in France. But from his £1.40 he must pay the cost of growing and harvesting the grapes, pressing them, fermenting the juice, clarifying and treating the wine. Then he must bottle, cork, encapsulate, label and pack the wine into cartons. If his margin after these direct costs is 50p, he's doing well.

The prime profiteer, however, is not the supermarket, even though it makes a healthy 97p in mark-up. It is the Chancellor who does best, by miles. Excise duty and VAT are two of the cheapest taxes to collect and from this single bottle of wine, the Treasury trousers a princely £1.84.

Travellers to wine-producing countries are always thrilled to find that by taking their own bottles, jugs or plastic casks to rustic vineyards offering wine on tap they can buy drinkable stuff for as little as 50p a litre. What too few travellers appreciate is that, for the wine itself, that's about what the supermarkets are paying for it. When enjoying your bargain bottle of wine, it is interesting to reflect on the economic reality known as 'added value' – which dictates that the worthiest person in the chain, the producer, has probably earned less than 10 per cent of the final price.

Cross-Channel Shopping

According to the Wine and Spirit Association, the British drink industry's trade body, one in seven bottles of wine consumed in Britain has been 'personally imported' by UK residents returning from the continent. The Association bases this figure on its own research, by quizzing motorists on the ferries about how much drink they are carrying.

So we can rely reasonably safely on this figure, which adds up to something like 200 million bottles a year. This is all wine on which the Chancellor won't collect a penny in excise duty or VAT and which displaces the wine British retailers might have sold, at modest profit, to the customers in question. No wonder the WSA gets in a spin about it.

But no amount of lobbying has made any difference to the Government's policy of continuing to rack up UK excise duty on wine – and thus making the attraction of booze-cruising progressively more attractive. Ferry companies and Eurotunnel are complicit. Outside the holiday seasons, they persistently offer day-return fares at mad prices to lure shoppers.

A chum and I did one run this year through the tunnel that cost £9 return for a car and up to five passengers. But in Calais, we got a bit of a surprise. We headed for the huge Auchan hypermarket, hitherto a source of extensive choice and deep bargains. But prices have escalated fearsomely since either of us was last here. Among the wines, bargains were sparse. Once, you could pick out decent southern *vins de pays* at well under £1 per bottle. Now, the cheapest wines are way above this mark, and I found none worth risking.

The best wine buys are among the *appellation contrôlée* ranks. A good choice from the Midi – Corbières, Minervois and so on – and lots of reds from the Rhône valley, especially from individually named villages. Familiar names such as Gigondas and Vacqueyras were expensive, but less renowned and equally good village wines from the likes of Cairanne and Vinsobres were keenly priced. Converting at the prevailing exchange rate of £1 to 1.4 euros, we paid between £2.85 and £3.48 for these, from the dependable 1999, 2000 and 2001 vintages. In the UK, they would cost £5 to £7.

There is plenty of ordinary dry white wine from the popular Loire appellations – from cheap Muscadet to pricey Sancerre – but I reckon typical saving was barely more than the £1.35 accounted for by the difference between UK and France excise duty and VAT.

And I was very disappointed by the Alsace wines. These are usually a real attraction, because they are sparse in England, and always expensive. But standard co-op wines that would be £6 in supermarkets here were close to £5 in Auchan.

If anything, the champagne offerings were worse. There used to be lots of interesting unknown brands at under £10. Now, nothing at all under that mark. I goggled at Heidsieck Blue Top at £13 in Auchan. The previous week, Somerfield had it on offer at £8.99. My own favourite, Veuve Clicquot Yellow Label was priced at £17. Okay, it's £22 in Britain, but in many merchants here, if you buy six, you'll get a discount down to £18 or £19.

I took a nosy look into the trolleys of the scores of English shoppers cruising the aisles, and noticed that no one at all was buying champagne. Before the euro came in, you expected to pay half UK price. Now, it seems, that particular bubble has popped.

It's much more fun to buy regional fizzes you hardly ever see in England – such as Crémant d'Alsace. The bottle I bought, a Blanc de Noir 2000 under Auchan's 'own label' name, Pierre Chanau (Chanau is a witty anagram of Auchan), was deliciously brisk and cost just £4.30. Also good value is Pyrenean fizz Blanquette de Limoux, costing as little as £3.

There were a couple of 'wine advisers' on duty in the store, offering tastings of wine and guiding shoppers, in English, to some of the wines on promotion. But with the greatest respect, I was unsure of the validity of the advice being offered.

My own advice is not to buy 'fine wine' from Bordeaux or Burgundy. Vintages on sale are almost universally too immature to drink now, and there is a proliferation of 1999 claret, which was a dismal year. What's more, anything priced above £15 would probably, believe it or not, be cheaper from a proper wine merchant in England.

There are quite a few non-French wines on offer in Auchan, but few bargains. The usual brands, such as Jacob's Creek and Blossom Hill, take up most of the space and are only about £1 to £1.50 off UK price.

Of course Auchan is a limited sample, but our experience does demonstrate some general trends. First, there is the inescapable fact that the value of sterling has slid by more than 15 per cent against that of the euro. The bottle of wine priced at 2 euros last year was really costing you £1.20. This year it's costing you £1.40.

And prices have most definitely been hiked in French supermarkets in the changeover from francs to euros – a lengthy but inexorable process of 'rounding up' that may have been overlooked by local shoppers, but was certainly noticeable to an occasional, and very price-conscious, visitor such as myself.

Prices are a lot less muddling, of course, if you take the conservative route and simply shop at a French-port branch of one of our own supermarket chains. Tesco's 'Vin Plus' branch in the immense Cité Europe shopping centre at the Pas de Calais (near the Eurotunnel terminal) is a place of pilgrimage for thousands of British shoppers, and likewise Sainsbury's lately expanded drinks shop across the way from the mega-Auchan we visited. Note, too that Majestic has taken over the former Wine and Beer Company, with branches in Calais, Cherbourg and Le Havre.

On the whole, by shopping in their French outposts, you save about £1.50 a bottle on the prices you would pay for the same table wines at home. So, if you buy five cases, you'll save £90. If this justifies the time and expense of getting across the Channel, then fine.

But it seems such a shame to go all the way to France and then just buy the same stuff you can get from your local supermarket back in Blighty. You'll save just as much money shopping in French supermarkets or wine warehouses, and have a lot more fun.

There is no limit to the quantity or value of goods you can bring back from any EU member country, provided it is not intended for resale in the UK. British Customs & Excise long ago published 'guidelines' as to what they consider are reasonable limits on drinks that can be deemed to be for 'personal consumption'. You can thus import, no questions asked, 90 litres of wine, 20 of fortified wine, ten of spirits and 110 of beer. That's about as much as a couple travelling together (and therefore able to import twice the above quantities) could cram into a family car without threatening the well-being of its suspension.

Savings on beer and spirits are, if anything, even more dramatic than they are on wine. French duty on beer is 5p a pint, compared to 33p here. This means a case of beer typically costing £12–£15 here can be had for under a fiver in Calais. It seems crazy. Similarly, a 70 cl bottle of London gin or Scotch whisky costing £11–£12 here is yours for £7–£8 in France, where duty on spirits is half the £5.48 charged here and mark-ups lower.

As if these differentials were not enough, the Channel ports also teem with good-value restaurants and hotels. Boulogne and Calais, Dieppe and Dunkirk bristle with venues where you can enjoy a £10–£15 menu of a standard that would set you back several times as much at home. And there are respectable hotels where a clean room with bath or shower, plus croissants and excellent coffee for breakfast, can be had for £25 all in.

Cork and Corks
– the Great Debate

I keep buying bottles of wine that turn out to be undrinkable because of the cork. In one week I had two bad bottles and it's beginning to get personal. I'm so cross I'll name names. One was Noble Road Shiraz 2001, costing £5.99 from Majestic. It smelled of mouldy sawdust and tasted vile. The other was Araldica Langhe Nebbiolo 1999, a reputable red from northern Italy, priced at £6.99 from Safeway. It should have given off a perfume of 'tar and roses' – the trademark of the Nebbiolo grape grown in the Langhe hills of Piedmont. But instead it reeked of something like wet mushrooms and tasted worse.

Both wines were ruined by what is called 246 trichloroanisol. TCA, as it's known with merciful brevity, is manifested by a horrible taint in the flavour of wine. It is caused by something called methylised trichlorophenol, which most commonly invades wine via poorly disinfected corks, although it's only fair to add that it can also get into the wine from infected barrels or cellar premises. The infection can get into natural corks at various stages in their production, perhaps into the bark of the tree itself. It can all seem rather vague, but one thing is for sure, TCA is an epidemic.

Who is to blame? The natural cork industry, centred on the cork oak forests of Portugal and Spain, is in the dock. Business has boomed for them in the last 20 years as demand for quality wines – those 'closed' with a cork and very often made for export – has burgeoned in markets like Britain, the US and the Far East. As the quantity of corks annually produced has spiralled into the billions, quality is alleged to have suffered.

Naturally, the cork farmers insist their standards are as high as ever. They admit they are aware of TCA and are working on eliminating it. And equally naturally, they claim the production of natural corks is a 'renewable process'. The cork oak tree lives up to 150 years and the outer bark that provides the raw material can be harvested – peeled off like the skin from an orange – every 10 years or so. The growers also claim their forests are a major source of employment in hard-pressed regions where there isn't much other work – and furthermore that the land sustains a variety of unique animal and plant species.

Manufacturers of the finished product, meanwhile, claim to be seeking a cure for TCA. Sabate, one of the biggest cork makers in France, has promised that within five years the billion corks it produces annually will all be guaranteed TCA-free, thanks to new technology.

But however persuasive the case might be for a natural product that has been made by traditional means in Europe for centuries, it looks as if it may be too late for the real-cork business. Wine producers around the world have already lost patience. As any wine drinker in Britain by now knows, plastic 'corks' now seal countless bottles from Australia, the US and South America. New World wine producers are not in the least sentimental about the long history of natural cork making in Europe, and plastics companies such as the US giant Supremecorq, founded barely a decade ago, have pioneered an entirely new industry in which good profits look set to be made.

Personally, I hate plastic – or more correctly polymer – corks. They are often difficult to extract, they are even more difficult to detach from the corkscrew afterwards and they are impossible to reinsert into the neck of the bottle.

But they are definitely not prone to TCA, or any of the other ailments, such as weevils, fissures or mould, to which their natural counterparts are so notoriously prone. Long-term tests by various institutions are currently under way to see if wine will keep in good condition for long periods with a polymer seal instead of a natural one, and so far, there is no evidence the plastic degenerates or taints the wine.

And now there is another alternative to the natural cork, and this is the one that looks most likely to win the day.

It's the screwcap, best known under the dominant trade name, Stelvin, which is exactly the same closure you find on bottles of spirits – a metal seal, lined with plastic. It is arguably a better seal than a polymer or natural cork because it closes right over the mouth of the bottle rather than merely obstructing the neck. And it is easy to open – no need for a corkscrew – and just as simple to reseal.

But for wine? What about the romance of drawing the cork, of that evocative 'pop' as it clears the bottle?

'The hell with it,' Bob McLean, one of the legends of Australian winemaking, told me when I met him at a tasting of his St Hallett wines during a recent UK promotional tour. 'If I can guarantee that none of my wines will be wrecked by cork taint, I'll be happy to chuck the corkscrew away for ever.'

Mr McLean was feeling understandably aggrieved at the time. Touring Britain to show off his wines – some of them very grand and expensive indeed – he had opened 30 bottles at one event along the way only to find that six of them were infected with TCA.

Ironically, Mr McLean's company had co-operated in an experiment with Tesco five years back in which some of their wines were specially bottled with screwcaps to see how customers reacted to them. 'But it didn't work out,' he said. 'People clearly felt any wine, however good, or for that matter expensive, would have to be nasty if it came with what looks like a cheap closure.'

St Hallett white wines, however, will soon be appearing in Tesco and at other outlets with screwcaps. Bob McLean and his colleagues have had enough of cork taint and are telling their customers so.

They won't have had any difficulty persuading Tesco. Britain's biggest wine retailer has taken screwcap wine to its heart, last year launching a large range of own-label bottles called 'Unwind' wines – all £4.99, and all with screwcaps.

'We now sell between 600,000 and 1.3 million bottles of premium screwcapped wines a month,' say Tesco. 'It seems that it was a risk worth taking and we have challenged the perception of screwcap equals cheap. It's now screwcap equals quality.'

They're not kidding. They are demanding that major suppliers like Australia's Southcorp (Lindemans, Penfolds and Rosemount brands) and Hardy's and US giant Gallo use screwcaps in place of natural corks. And they are welcoming screwcaps from all kinds of producers. At this year's Tesco tasting, I was impressed with an elegant Chablis Premier Cru from one of France's most revered winemakers, Michel Laroche and priced at £13.99 – complete with screwcap.

In New Zealand, the screwcap is already king. Leading producers such as Villa Maria have rejected corks altogether and formed a movement called the New Zealand Screwcap Wine Seal Initiative, declaring: 'We are committed to bringing our wines to you in the best possible condition. And we know that the only way to do this confidently is to seal every bottle with a screwcap wine seal.'

There is some customer resistance to the trend. The Consumers' Association has published a survey of both the wine trade and the wine-buying public in which it found that while two-thirds of people in the trade think the screwcap will catch on, two-thirds of wine shoppers disagree, saying the traditional cork is something they would miss.

But I can't really see a Save the Cork campaign getting under way. If the wine producers and retailers want screwcaps – for all but the tiny number of 'fine wines' that are made for very long keeping – I don't believe they will show any mercy to the natural cork industry.

Tesco's own words on this subject will surely strike fear into the heart of anyone who depends for their living on making corks. 'We want our customers to get their wine in the best condition possible and cork cannot guarantee that.'

The Supermarket
Best Wine Buys

First, a short explanation of my scoring system. As an entirely subjective guide to relative value among the wines mentioned in the book, I use a scoring scale of 0 to 10. In the notes I took while tasting, I gave each wine a score within this range, and just about all the wines that were given a score of 7 and above are included. Wines scoring 6 and under are mostly left out, because this is not a book in which there is space to decry wines I have not liked.

I would recommend any of the wines with a score of 7 or above. Those scoring 7 are those I account good wines at a fair price. A score of 8 signifies a very good wine at a fair price and a score of 9 indicates special quality and value. Those that earn 10 out of 10 are, obviously enough, the wines I don't think can be bettered.

Out of the dozens I have tasted, just 30 wines scored the maximum 10 out of 10 on my personal scale. They are listed overleaf. A good number of them are very inexpensive and are rated so highly because they seemed to me quite remarkable value for money. If it really signifies anything, it might be of interest to point out that the number of top scores was highest from Waitrose, with 12, followed by four from Marks & Spencer and three each from Majestic and Sainsbury's. Countries of origin are led by France and Spain, each with eight top scores, four for Australia, then Argentina and South Africa, each with three.

My Top 30 Supermarket Wines

Red Wines

£3.19	Cuvée des Amandiers 2002	France	Majestic
£3.69	Saumur Les Nivières 2002	France	Waitrose
£3.79	Coldridge Estate Shiraz 2002	Australia	Majestic
£3.99	Argentine Tempranillo 2002	Argentina	Somerfield
£3.99	Maximo Tempranillo 2000	Spain	Safeway
£3.99	M Red Rioja	Spain	Morrisons
£3.99	Somerton Shiraz-Cabernet-Merlot 2002	Australia	Waitrose
£3.99	Viña Fuerte Garnacha 2002	Spain	Waitrose
£4.99	Fairtrade Cape Trinity 2002	South Africa	Co-op
£4.99	Las Almenas Crianza 2000	Spain	Marks & Spencer
£5.99	Botteghino Chianti 2001	Italy	Marks & Spencer
£5.99	Excelsior Estate Paddock Shiraz 2002	South Africa	Waitrose
£17.99	Réserve de la Comtesse 1997	France	Sainsbury's

White Wines

£2.99	Bianco Beneventano 2002	Italy	Marks & Spencer
£2.99	Broken Bridge Chardonnay-Colombard 2002	Australia	Waitrose
£4.79	Alsace Pinot Blanc Preiss Zimmer 2001	France	Morrisons
£4.99	Atlantique Sauvignon Blanc 2002	France	Sainsbury's
£4.99	Muscadet Côtes de Grandlieu sur Lie, Fief Guérin 2002	France	Waitrose

£4.99	Tempus Two Chardonnay 2002	Australia	Tesco
£5.49	Torres Viña Esmeralda 2002	Spain	Somerfield and Waitrose
£5.99	Sauternes La Fleur d'Or 1999	France	Safeway
£5.99	Urziger Würzgarten Riesling Spätlese, Christoffel-Berres 1992	Germany	Majestic
£5.99	Villa Wolf Pinot Gris 2001	Germany	Sainsbury's
£7.99	Château Carsin Cuvée Prestige 2001	France	Waitrose
£7.99	Jordan Chardonnay 2002	South Africa	Waitrose
£7.99	Kaituna Hills Reserve Sauvignon Blanc 2002	New Zealand	Marks & Spencer
£9.99	Catena Agrelo Vineyards Chardonnay 2001	Argentina	Waitrose

Fortified Wines

£3.87	Asda Manzanilla sherry	Spain	Asda
£5.99	Solera Jerezana Dry Amontillado sherry	Spain	Waitrose
£5.99	Waitrose Solera Jerezana Dry Oloroso sherry	Spain	Waitrose

Aldi

I have tasted just a handful of Aldi wines this year and remarked, as before, on how cheap they are. The German company has more than 250 stores in the UK – a fraction of its worldwide network of 5,000 branches – and so it must have monster buying power. Unlike Lidl, its immediate rival at the 'no-frills' end of the supermarket business, Aldi has a range of own-label wines, which it is steadily increasing in scope. A source of bargains to watch.

If you don't know where your nearest Aldi is, ring the Store Location Line on 08705 134262 or look on the web at **www.aldi-stores.co.uk**

RED WINES   UNDER £3

AUSTRALIA

8 **Badger Creek Shiraz Cabernet 2002**   £2.99
Jammy Australian berry bomb with 14.5 per cent alcohol
at an incredible price – okay, it's unsophisticated stuff,
but has no outright faults and constitutes a proper
bargain.

CHILE

7 **Chilean Cabernet Sauvignon**   £2.99
Open this wine in advance and decant it – into another
(clean) wine bottle if you haven't any kind of decanter –
because aeration improves it measurably. It's a purple-
bright young wine with lots of briary fruit that blooms in
the glass and goes a treat with chilli dishes.

FRANCE

7 **Claret 'Château Selection' 2001**   £2.99
'Perfectly drinkable' said one taster at the little gathering
I held to try Aldi's wines, and that seemed fair comment.
This is extremely cheap but it isn't nasty and is certainly
as good as other supermarket generic Bordeaux costing a
lot more – so if it has to be claret, and it has to be under
£3, it has to be Aldi.

SPAIN

8 **Campo Lindo Crianza 2000**   £2.99
Lightweight, oaky red has that Spanish style familiar from
bargain brands like Don Darias – with a considerable
price advantage in this case.

RED WINES   £3 TO £5

FRANCE

9 Château Calbet, Cabardes 2001   £3.99
Excellent, ripe (13.5 per cent alcohol), quality dark-fruit Languedoc red at a very keen price. Smart-looking, genuine bargain.

DRY WHITE WINES   UNDER £3

GERMANY

7 Budavar Chardonnay 2002   £2.49
The cheapest bottle of wine in the book is a thoroughly decent, rather heavyweight (13 per cent alcohol), dry and flavoursome recognisable Chardonnay bottled by the giant St Ursula co-operative in Germany – in a utilitarian screwcap bottle. I promise, this is perfectly good wine, and I cannot fathom how Aldi can make any money from it at such a price.

DRY WHITE WINES   £3 TO £5

FRANCE

**8 Chablis 'La Larme d'Or', Jean Louis
Quinson 2002   £4.99**
The only Chablis under a fiver in the universe? It's not at all bad – the right flinty whiff and a lot of forceful Chardonnay flavour here, with an assertive acidity that suggests it will last.

Asda

The former Associated Dairies supermarket chain, now part of the world's biggest retailer, US giant Wal-Mart, is said to be the fastest-growing of all retailers in Britain. It has 250-odd outlets throughout the UK – fewer than half the number of branches of Sainsbury or Tesco – but is expected before long to overtake Sainsbury's in terms of sales.

The wine range at Asda is large and bewildering. There are hordes of the usual ubiquitous brands from Australia and America at the same price (give or take a penny or two) as everywhere else. But there is also an ill-defined range of exclusive own-label wines, many of which are of inspired quality and cheaper than their approximate counterparts in the other Big Four supermarkets.

As part of a company with huge buying power – Wal-Mart's annual sales are £150 billion – Asda no doubt has considerable negotiating strength when it comes to dealing with suppliers worldwide. The chain reckons that its merchandise, based on a sample of 1,600 products, is on average 12 per cent cheaper than among its major rivals.

So, if you're a particularly price-sensitive shopper for wine, Asda merits a look. In common with other supermarkets, it offers a discount of five per cent on 'bulk' buys – which in this case means six or more bottles of wine (including vermouth and fortified wine) priced at £2.50 or above. And again in common with the competition, Asda does regular promotions on both branded and own-label wines. Price, I must confess, looks to be the main attraction on the wine front, as few of the bottles I have tried over the last year have scored much for interest.

RED WINES · UNDER £3

ARGENTINA

7 **Asda Argentinian Red** £2.52
This is even lighter than I remember from last year and probably from a new source. It's just short of tasting too much of boiled sweets, but it is quite remarkably cheap (same label cost £2.97 a year ago) and will do for parties, sangria and so forth.

RED WINES · £3 TO £5

ARGENTINA

8 **Far Flung Cabernet-Merlot 2001** £4.50
A perennial good buy at Asda, this is a quality wine with good intensity of blackcurrant and sweet-morello fruit.

FRANCE

8 **La Chasse du Pape, Gabriel Meffre 2001** £4.38
Ubiquitous Côtes du Rhône masquerading as Châteauneuf du Pape – dense and grippingly good with spice and warmth – and at a keen price from Asda.

8 **Rasteau Côtes du Rhône Villages 2001** £4.52
Hurry out to sample this grippy and darkly spicy CdR from an excellent vintage and at a price that seems certain to rise with the 2002, which is likely to be less good.

S AFRICA

8 **Dumisani Pinotage-Shiraz 2002** £3.52
Good-value juicy Cape red is founded in the national grape, Pinotage, imparting distinctive redcurrant fruit, plus noticeable peppery warmth from the Shiraz.

RED WINES   OVER £5

AUSTRALIA

🍷8 Pencil Pine Chambourcin 2001   £6.01
You have to give credit to Asda for listing such an oddity
as this – and at such an odd price, too. The hybrid
Chambourcin vine celebrated its 40th birthday in 2003,
and is mainly planted in the Loire Valley, but is doing just
fine Down Under, too, here making a bright, squishy-
fruit, youthful-tasting yet Aussie-ripe red of real
distinction.

CHILE

🍷8 Cono Sur Pinot Noir 2001   £5.02
Ripe, raspberry perfume rises from this alluring, earthily
delicious Pinot, which makes a rare success of rendering
this difficult grape into a wine of concentration and
character. 2002 is equally good.

🍷8 Terramater Zinfandel-Shiraz 2000   £5.02
Unusual blend delivers a big, soft-fruit red that manages
to combine brambliness with a note of silk.

FRANCE

🍷8 Fitou Reserve La Montagne 2000   £5.01
A gripping dark ripe and maturing example of the
perpetually popular Fitou formula.

DRY WHITE WINES   £3 TO £5

ARGENTINA

♆8   Asda Argentinian Torrontes 2002   £3.51
It's very much a matter of taste, but I think the native Torrontes grape of the Mendoza region makes fascinating dry wine – a sort of soft, Alsacien style with overtones of Muscat and spice and refreshing qualities, too. This one is straightforward and good value.

AUSTRALIA

♆8   Oxford Landing Chardonnay 2002   £4.46
Good price for this popular brand, which is always an interesting and rather exotic glassful, with pineappley fruit and the power to refresh.

♆7   Yellow Tail Chardonnay 2002   £4.88
Named after the yellowtail kangaroo and with apposite designer label, this has tropical-peachy fruit and the coconut background imparted by use of oak chips in the fermenting tanks. It's jumping off the shelves in America, where it is the biggest-selling of all imported wines, and may well take off over here too.

FRANCE

♆8   Denis Marchais Hand Picked Vouvray 2001 £4.88
I must persist in recommending this particularly fresh and zesty Loire off-dry white, which has a background of honeysuckle on both aroma and flavour.

HUNGARY

♆7   Riverview Chardonnay Pinot Grigio 2002   £3.98
A grape blend like this looks like a bid to please everyone, but it works well enough, with the PG's trademark spice backed up by a gratifyingly forceful, creamy weight from the Chardonnay.

ITALY

🍷 **8** San Marco Orvieto Abboccato 2001 £3.47
I was very pleased to see this, the original 'soft' style of
Umbria's now very popular tourist town of Orvieto – a
really sunny and aromatic off-dry white, and cheap.

DRY WHITE WINES	OVER £5

NEW ZEALAND

🍷 **9** Montana Unoaked East Coast
Chardonnay 2002 £6.00
This is a glittering wine, lemon-gold in colour and with a
matching citrussy background to the lively, pineapple
fruit. It echoes the unique fresh-yet-intense style that so
marks out New Zealand's great Sauvignon wines, and as
such is another happy variation on this ever-extending
theme.

S AFRICA

🍷 **9** Porcupine Ridge Sauvignon Blanc 2002 £4.98
I would like to say this has prickly fruit or something but
I had better stick to the point and report that it is a
deliciously lively and brisk, grassy-fresh Sauvignon of
real quality – and at a very good price at Asda.

FORTIFIED WINES	£3 TO £5

SPAIN

🍷 **10** Asda Manzanilla sherry £3.87
A terrific buy at this price, here is a textbook bone-dry
pale sherry for drinking cold out of a decent-sized glass,
lovely tangy and aromatic refresher of a quality to match
pricier brands. **BEST BUY**

Co-op

As supermarkets go, the Co-op can hardly lay claim to the most prestigious image. But the wines in the 1,800 or so licensed convenience stores and larger outlets are nevertheless very well chosen.

Even in small Co-op branches you will find a decent choice of real-quality wines, and in the superstores the selection will run into hundreds of different lines.

A feature of all the own-brand wines is their back labels. It is the Co-op's policy to state all the ingredients in their own wines, and the back labels look very busy on account of it. Co-op Australian Merlot, for example, boasts this ingredient list: 'Grapes. Tartaric acid, Tannin, Preservative (Sulphur dioxide). Made using: Yeast, Yeast nutrient (Diammonium phosphate), Copper sulphate, Carbon dioxide, Nitrogen. Cleared using: Filtration, Gelatine, Pectinolytic enzymes.'

Nothing sinister among this lot, I promise, but in an ingredient-conscious world, the Co-op should be congratulated on this kind of openness. No other supermarket – and certainly no other wine retailer, including organic-wine specialists – is similarly upfront, and I hope the Co-op is winning lots of new customers on account of it.

Old-fashioned though it may sound, the Co-op Dividend scheme is a real money-saver, particularly on high-unit-value items such as bottles of wine. 'Co-op Dividend is the most generous supermarket loyalty card, paying twice as much on average as other food retailers' schemes,' declares the Co-op's manifesto. 'Cardholders earn cash back on all their purchases – triple dividend of 3p for every £1 spent on Co-op brand goods ...'

The Co-op has its own dedicated website – **www.co-opdrinks2u.com** – for wine shoppers who prefer home delivery. It gives details of current special offers as well as 'a selection' from the full list of 500-or-so different wines and spirits. If you're not online, you can also telephone co-opdrinks2u on freephone 0800 083 0501.

RED WINES	UNDER £3

ITALY

8 **Co-op Sicilian Red** £2.99
Well up to average for the species, this is a good, heathery Sicilian with a little bit of sweetness that is not unlikeable – and one of the few still under the £3 mark.

RED WINES	£3 TO £5

ARGENTINA

7 **Argento Malbec 2002** £4.99
Solid, dark and consistent brand by the estimable Nicolas Catena has the leather and dark chocolate grip that thoroughly typifies Argentine Malbec.

AUSTRALIA

8 **Co-op Merlot South East Australia 2002** £4.79
Surprisingly sleek, cherry-scented and artfully balanced sweetly ripe (14 per cent alcohol) red from a grape that doesn't normally do all that well Down Under. Easy-drinking and good value.

CHILE

8 **Fairtrade Carmenère 2001** £4.99
Dense, ripe, dark red from the Los Robles winery where the Fairtrade scheme operates to ensure workers are fairly paid.

9 **Co-op Vin de Pays Merlot** £3.79
This is consistently great value, though a tad pricier than last year, with its berry-burst of ripe uninhibited southern fruit and satisfying weight and finish.

8 **Co-op Fitou 2001** £3.99
This is a really cracking, brightly ripe and bracing, summer-fruit red from the ever-dependable Mont Tauch co-operative that made Fitou the first famous appellation of Languedoc-Roussillon 25 years ago. Marvellous bargain.

8 **Château Pierrousselle 2000** £4.99
At the time of writing there was still some of this left, and I recommend getting out after it, as it is a properly rounded-out claret with pleasing weight, purity of soft, plump fruit and crisp finish.

7 **Co-op Chianti 2001** £3.79
Handsome label (by Botticelli no less) might suggest this very cheap Chianti wouldn't live up to expectations, but it is perfectly good, demonstrating the right style of cherry fruit and dry finish, with enough weight to carry the day.

7 **Co-op Puglia Primitivo-Sangiovese 2001** £4.29
Gripping, brambly red has lots of interest for the money – apparently it is one of the Co-op's best-selling wines.

7 **Big Baga 2001** £4.49
In case you're lured into this by the name, fear not, as it's a decent darkly juicy red with more than a hint of sweetness, redeemed by an interestingly arid finish.

FRANCE

ITALY

PORTUGAL

10 Fairtrade Cape Trinity 2002   £4.99

Putting aside any socio-political motives one might have for liking this wine, which is made under the Fairtrade scheme, this is a sweetie of a wine in its own right – lush, plummy and juicy middleweight red from a trinity of Cabernets (Franc, Sauvignon and Ruby) and showing what with justifiable comment the back label calls 'distinctly South African flavours'.   **BEST BUY**

9 Goats do Roam 2002   £4.99

Terrific, deliciously yielding, but robust, firm and ripe bargain red is made largely from South Africa's indigenous grape variety, the Pinotage. The odd name is a tilt at French Côtes du Rhône but also celebrates the fact that the maker, Charles Back, is a goat farmer as well. A herd of 600 of them roam his Fairview estate, and some of South Africa's best cheese is made from their milk.

8 Jilly Goolden Keynote Shiraz 2002   £4.99

Dare I risk my own adjectives on the creation of the mistress of the vinous metaphor? Best not. But this wine scores 8 because it is good – generous and satisfying, and not as inflated in price as might be expected of any product with a celebrity endorsement.

SOUTH AFRICA

RED WINES   **OVER £5**

8 Co-op Chianti Classico 2001   £6.49

Splendid gaudy label belies the serious quality of this thoroughly likeable middleweight with all the cherry-raspberry smell and grippy, almondy fruit you hope for in a decent Chianti, and at a realistic price.

ITALY

SPAIN

8 **Berberana Carta de Oro Rioja**
Reserva 1998 £6.99
Classic old-fashioned Rioja with silky vanilla texture and
profound cassis depths for serious contemplation.
Mature enough to enjoy now, but will round out further
if kept a year or two.

DRY WHITE WINES £3 TO £5

AUSTRALIA

7 **Yellow Tail Chardonnay 2002** £4.99
Named after the yellowtail kangaroo and with apposite
designer label, this has tropical-peachy fruit and the
coconut background imparted by use of oak chips in the
fermenting tanks. It's jumping off the shelves in America,
where it is the biggest-selling of all imported wines, and
may well take off over here too.

HUNGARY

7 **Riverview Chardonnay Pinot Grigio 2002** £3.99
A grape blend like this looks like a bid to please
everyone, but it works well enough, with the PG's
trademark spice backed up by a gratifyingly forceful
creamy weight from the Chardonnay.

NEW ZEALAND

7 **Nobilo White Cloud 2002** £4.99
The Co-op has long persisted with this old-fashioned
Kiwi white, made from the Muller-Thurgau grapes that
are a mainstay of disdained German Liebfraumilch and
once filled the vineyards of New Zealand – before
Sauvignon Blanc and Chardonnay took over. White
Cloud is a well-made wine, though, soft and grapey (it
has a bit of Muscat in it) rather than sweet, and yet with
good clean acidity. Just the ticket for the more cautious,
dare I say untrained, palate.

Majestic

You don't need to be a genius at riddles to spot that Majestic is the odd one out in this guide – by virtue of the fact that it is not a supermarket. But here's a pretext – Majestic supplies its customers with supermarket trolleys, because the minimum purchase from their 'warehouse' branches is a dozen bottles of wine (any mix) at a time.

And anyway, the wines at Majestic are simply too good to be left out of any guide. The 105-branch chain has a unique range, far and away better than any other high-street off-licence retailer – including Oddbins – and at prices that can be described as advantageous.

All the prices mentioned here are standard list prices, but at any time you will find a large proportion of them reduced, because Majestic is forever doing 'multibuy' offers. You know the sort of thing: buy two bottles of X, usually £4.99, and pay £3.99 each. Given that you'll be buying 12 or more bottles at a time, this kind of discount makes a lot of sense – and reduces the typical bill in Majestic (which I gather is £105 per customer) very usefully indeed.

I enjoy shopping in Majestic, but do always look at its regularly updated and well-presented lists first, because it's all too easy to miss out on particular wines when you're confronted with the canyons of them that form the aisles in the shops – which are, indeed, just straightforward warehouse-style spaces. Majestic seems to specialise in taking over former car showrooms, and this seems poetic justice to me.

Although Majestic continues to expand its network across Britain, the company has decided not to open any more branches in the region of south-east England within easiest reach of the Channel ports. Wholesaling wine in competition with the supermarkets and booze warehouses across the water is a lost cause. So instead of investing in hugely expensive sites in Kent or East Sussex, Majestic has spent £4 million on the four-branch Calais business prosaically known as the Wine and Beer Company.

Over time, the shops – two in Calais and one each in Cherbourg and Le Havre – will take on more and more of Majestic's own range, but will retain many of the bog-standard booze-cruise Liebfraumilches and branded wines that have been its mainstay to date. If you're planning a trip you can preview the list and its mass of special offers online either at **www.wineandbeer.co.uk** or, if French bureaucracy has permitted, on Majestic's own brilliantly ordered site at **www.majestic.co.uk**. You can even order all the wines you want online, and simply turn up to collect the goods when the time comes.

Finally, a confession. I missed the Majestic tasting this year – for genuinely unavoidable reasons – and that's why this section is a bit shorter than it should be. All the wines reported on are bottles I bought. In fact they are all the bottles I bought, and that all were well worthy of description shows just how consistently good Majestic is across the board – at least at the price levels I can afford.

RED WINES   UNDER £3

FRANCE

9 **Cuvée de Richard Rouge 2002**   £2.99
Majestic's house red, a Vin de Pays de l'Aude is as good
in this vintage as ever – lively, juicy young red without
fault and an outstanding bargain.

RED WINES   £3 TO £5

ARGENTINA

7 **Argento Malbec 2002**   £4.99
Solid, dark and consistent brand by the estimable Nicolas
Catena has the leather and dark chocolate grip that
thoroughly typifies Argentine Malbec.

AUSTRALIA

10 **Coldridge Estate Shiraz 2002**   £3.79
Majestic 'house' Aussie Shiraz is quite brilliant, being
possessed of all the darkness, warmth and grip you
anticipate from the genre, but balancing it up with a deft
purity and straightforwardness that suggests a cooler-
climate wine – really super stuff at a very keen price.
BEST BUY

FRANCE

10 **Cuvée des Amandiers 2002**   £3.19
Up this year from £2.99 but still a tremendously good
buy, this Vin de Pays d'Oc is dashingly fruity, well-
rounded, blackcurrant and in every way tastes well
above its very low price – marvellous buy.   **BEST BUY**

8 **Corbières Terra Vitis 2001**   £4.99
From the Mont Tauch co-operative in Fitou, this wine
comes from 'environmentally friendly vineyards' and is a
good, gutsy, darkly ripe and minty, muscular red.

PORTUGAL

8   Dão Duque de Viseu 2000   **£4.99**
Dark, minty red from unfashionable Dão region has that
nice suggestion of eucalyptus that crops up in so many
Portuguese wines, and offers a distinctive range of taste
sensations you don't get elsewhere. Made with the same
grapes that go into port.

8   Tuera Douro Tinto 1999   **£4.99**
Typical Douro table red with porty style and the major
added attraction of maturity – an elegant, minty glassful
of real character.

RED WINES   OVER £5

ARGENTINA

8   Catena Cabernet Sauvignon 2000   **£5.99**
I am a great fan of this perennially stylish Cabernet, with
its clarety hints of tobacco and silk combined with the
precocious ripeness and bounce that Catena always
manages to contrive.

AUSTRALIA

7   Noble Road Shiraz 2001   **£5.99**
'Knocks your socks off,' said one taster of this intense but
nicely weighted, pure-blackberry smoothie. One bottle
was horribly corky, though the other was fine – but do
beware that bad corks come in batches.

**7   St Hallett Gamekeepers
Grenache-Shiraz 2002**   **£5.99**
Famed Barossa Valley vineyard adopts some rather odd
brand names but makes consistently brilliant wines at
what seem very fair prices for Australia. This is a richly
concentrated, dark-fruit blend but has a light touch.

AUSTRALIA

**8 Wolf Blass Shiraz
Cabernet Sauvignon 2001** £6.49
Lovely, silky, rich blend of blackcurrant and spice in this masterly middleweight from the vineyard founded 35 years ago by German immigrant Wolfgang Blass. A well-known brand, but not one that is resting on its laurels.

8 Tyrrells Old Winery Pinot Noir 2002 £6.99
Australia usually struggles to make decent Pinot but this hits the spot – proper strawberry-cherry smell and that authentic silkiness.

9 Tatachilla Grenache-Shiraz 2001 £7.49
Gorgeous, squashed-fruit nose on this crushed-bramble, lavishly ripe and maturing blend from the McLaren Vale, with an epic 14.5 per cent alcohol.

7 Kangarilla Road Shiraz 2001 £8.99
Powerful, meaty-spicy, red wine from a producer long favoured by Majestic.

CHILE

**8 Santa Rita Cabernet Sauvignon
Reserva 2001** £6.99
Dark and firmly fruity, young-tasting, immediately appealing, oaked mid-heavyweight with 14 per cent alcohol is somehow effortlessly pleasing – a well-judged wine.

7 Santa Rita Merlot Reserva 2001 £6.99
Black-cherry sweetness balanced by firm, mouth-gripping dryness in this subtly oaked special edition of Santa Rita's perennially decent Merlot.

Majestic

FRANCE

8 **Marsannay Rouge Louis Latour 2000** £7.49
A delicious introduction to the summer-fruit, earthily
appealing classic style of red Burgundy wine, from Pinot
Noir grapes, and for once at a reasonable price.

9 **Château de Gaudou Cuvée Renaissance,**
Cahors 2000 £7.99
I bought a bottle of this meaning to keep it, because the
bottle of the 1999 vintage I bought needed keeping, too,
but out of a sense of duty (who said anything about
impatient thirst?) I opened it anyway and it's even better
than the 1999, again fabulously dense and velvety and
with subtler oaking and tingling spice. A gorgeous wine
from Cahors' best estate. But here's the catch – it would
have been a lot better if I had left it another year before
opening!

8 **Domaine des Ducs, St Amour 2001** £7.99
This is the true expression of the vigorous, juicy Gamay-
grape style of this unique red wine, in this case from a great
estate in the highly rated Beaujolais village of St Amour.

7 **Morgon Jean Descombes,**
Georges Duboeuf 2002 £7.99
Majestic are great promoters of the wines of 'King of
Beaujolais' Georges Duboeuf and this one, from the
much-rated cru of Morgon is a good one with firmly set
but gushing flavours in the proper, uniquely stimulating
Beaujolais style.

SPAIN

7 **Mas Collet Celler de Capçanes 2000** £5.99
Spirity nose on a big, spicy-fiery red of character with 14
per cent alcohol and satisfying aftertaste – for the macho
drinker, good with suitably heated Mexican food.

ROSÉ WINES	£3 TO £5

FRANCE

**7 Château Guiot Rosé,
Costières de Nîmes 2002** £4.99

Pale magenta colour but a strong strawberry perfume from this sunny and fresh pink glugger from the estimable appellation of Nîmes in the Midi.

ROSÉ WINES	OVER £5

FRANCE

9 Château de Sours Rosé 2002 £7.49

Seven quid is a lot of money for a rosé but this Bordeaux is worth it, a true luxury pink with lavish cherry-and-blossom perfume, stacks of serious summery fruit and textbook acidity with the power to refresh and stimulate – best pink I've tasted all year.

DRY WHITE WINES	UNDER £3

FRANCE

8 Cuvée de Richard Blanc 2002 £2.99

Consistent house white is fresh without being sharp, a low-acid party wine from the region of Toulouse in the deep south.

DRY WHITE WINES	£3 TO £5

AUSTRALIA

8 Coldridge Estate Semillon-Chardonnay 2002 £3.49

Jolly cheap, a compromise wine not as good as the straight Chardonnay (see immediately below) but a crowd-pleaser with agreeable tropical aroma and peachy fruit.

9 Coldridge Estate Chardonnay 2002 £3.79

I will admit that this brightly fresh wine scores as highly for affordability as it does for nuance of aroma or flavour, but it is a perfectly good Aussie Chardy – as good as most at, say, £4.99 – and thus constitutes a real bargain.

AUSTRALIA

8 **Oxford Landing Chardonnay 2002** £4.99
Majestic loyally follows this brand and with reason, because it is always an interesting and rather exotic glassful, with pineappley fruit and the power to refresh.

FRANCE

8 **Sauvignon de Touraine,**
Domaine de La Prévoté 2002 £4.99
Majestic seems to be expanding its range from the Loire more than any other part of the list, and I hope this signifies a long-term trend. This 'entry-price' Sauvignon from the region is a very good introduction indeed, with lots of tangy interest.

ITALY

8 **Cavalchina Bianco di Custoza 2002** £4.99
Floral nose and plenty of glittering fruit in this delicate, but emphatically fruity, Veronese dry white in the style of better-known Soave.

DRY WHITE WINES   OVER £5

7 **Bethany Riesling 2002** £5.99
I believe Bethany wines have been better in earlier vintages, but liked this one for its vegetal-limey style with tangy-flinty notes. The maker reckons it will 'no doubt improve in depth and complexity after a few years of careful cellaring'.

AUSTRALIA

8 **Yalumba Barossa Chardonnay 2002** £6.99
At first it seems a conventional Barossa Chardy, very ripe (14 per cent alcohol) and rich, but it dawns that here, too, is a lifting limey acidity, which gives it a distinctive classy balance and interest – a textbook, pure-varietal wine worth seeking out.

AUSTRALIA

8 Yalumba Y Viognier 2002 £6.99

Terrific perfume on this wine has notes of brown sugar, apricots and honeysuckle, and lots of sleek, soft and insinuating exotic fruit in the mouth. Very easy to drink with posh seafood or as a stand-alone wine, but be aware of its 14 per cent alcohol.

FRANCE

8 Quincy Le Rimonet, Joseph Mellot 2001 £5.99

This vintage might be sold out by now, but it is such a likeable, tangy and distinctive Sauvignon it should be sought out – and I'd take a chance on the 2002 vintage (good in the Loire) if it's in.

7 Alsace Tokay Pinot Gris, Bott-Geyl 2000 £9.99

Gold-coloured, lush, smoky-spicy classic wine of great character I tasted last time round and has lingered – which can only be a good thing as these wines improve over time. Would score 8 but Majestic have had the effrontery to up the price since last time.

GERMANY

9 Burg Layer Schlossberg, Michael Schäfer, Riesling Spätlese 1990 £5.49

In its thirteenth year this Moselle is just beginning to show its age with a gold colour and whiff of the intriguing 'petrol' scent given off by maturing Riesling. There are butterscotch notes in the depths of the keen, appley flavours and still plenty of vigour.

10 Urziger Würzgarten Riesling Spätlese, Christoffel-Berres 1992 £5.99

11-year-old Moselle as fresh and lush as meadow grass with divine Granny Smith nose and tearaway, tingly, ripe Riesling fruit – a wine of astonishing maturity and wonderment (and just 8 per cent alcohol) for the same price as some ineffably boring Australian global brand.
BEST BUY

Majestic

GERMANY

8 **Urziger Würzgarten Riesling Auslese,**
Christoffel-Berres 1997 £6.99
Sublime crisp and spritzy, apple-strudel Moselle with a
thrilling note of honeysuckle – not a cerebral Riesling,
perhaps, but a delicious refresher with a long finish of
insinuating sweetness.

NEW ZEALAND

8 **Oyster Bay Sauvignon Blanc 2002** £6.99
Zesty yet well-concentrated Kiwi classic from the lower
reaches of what can sometimes seem a rather steeply
ascending price scale.

7 **Villa Maria Sauvignon Blanc 2002** £7.99
The Marlborough estate of Villa Maria makes one of the
world's great Sauvignons. In this vintage, asparagus is
very much to the fore on the nose and in the fruit – right
through. A huge, ripe (13 per cent alcohol) stand-alone
or fish-matching wine worth the money. Screwcap bottle.

Marks & Spencer

 Jane Masters MW, whom I suspect of being largely responsible for the astonishing improvement in M&S's wines over recent years, has left the wine department to take charge of what the company calls the 'Flowers and Plants Category'. She says it is 'an ideal opportunity for a change and some personal growth'. If this wasn't M&S, I would assume she was trying to be funny, or ironic, or something. Becoming an MW (Master of Wine) is incredibly laborious and time-consuming – 'It makes a PhD look like a picnic,' one candidate told me – so why Ms Masters should walk away from wine I cannot possibly imagine. But Marks is a law unto itself. Ms Masters's job has gone to Edward Goodman, whose qualification for it appears to be that he has just spent two years running the aforementioned Flowers and Plants Category.

For the moment, though, the wines are looking very good and although all are exclusive M&S brands, there seems to be more choice than ever at the lower end of the price scale – an unexpected development at a retailer whose food and drink is hardly renowned for cheapness.

RED WINES   UNDER £3

FRANCE

8   **Gamay Vin de Pays de l'Ardèche 2002**   £2.99
Cheap, cherry-fruit red from the grape better known for
Beaujolais is a very respectable jug wine – the sort bistros
sell as house plonk for £10.

RED WINES   £3 TO £5

AUSTRALIA

8   **Pheasant Gully Bin 346**
Cabernet-Merlot 2002   £4.99
Lots of bright, edgy fruit – and 14 per cent alcohol – in
this lively blend.

8   **Pheasant Gully Bin 201**
Shiraz-Cabernet 2002   £4.99
Obvious oak but not to the point of masking the sunny
berry fruit. Very much a standard blend, but the price is
keen.

FRANCE

9   **Old Vines Grenache Noir 2001**   £4.99
Stalky whiff from this Roussillon red indicates the nifty
brightness of flavour that balances its very hearty and
gripping fruit – and prodigious 14.5 per cent alcohol.

8   **Visan Côtes du Rhône Villages 2001**   £4.99
Nice, peppery, budget wine with structure and length – a
lot of wine for the money.

ITALY

9   **Nero d'Avola-Syrah 2002**   £4.49
From Sicily, a brilliant dense, dark, berry-fruit red with a
lovely tarry centre and soft, pulpy flavours – a fascinating
wine for this price.

7 **Safra Nova 2001** £3.99
Ribatejo red with summer-fruit flavours and a good heart.

8 **Solorico 2001** £4.99
From the Ribatejo, this is made from the Aragones grape – the same as the Tempranillo of Spain – and has recognisable deep, blackcurrant flavours with a good structure and smoothness, finishing with a softly tannic dryness.

8 **Rockridge Merlot 2002** £4.99
Friendly, rustic, characterful, oaked, black-cherry red of real charm, and 14.5 per cent alcohol – perfect glugging.

8 **Spanish Red (1 litre)** £3.99
M&S house red is equivalent to £3 per 75 cl bottle and is good value for a bright, blackcurrant-perfumed, strawberry-fruit red of very acceptable quality.

8 **Campo Aldea Tempranillo 2001** £4.99
Luminous colour to this lively, young-tasting, hedgerow Rioja.

10 **Las Almenas Crianza 2000** £4.99
From Utiel-Requena in the hinterland of Valencia, a cracker of a red wine, dense in colour and with a smell deliciously evocative of newly plucked, sun-ripened brambles. It's a real mouthfiller, with firm bright briary fruit that goes right through to a clean, lingering finish.
BEST BUY

ARGENTINA

7 **Canale Merlot Reserve 2001** £9.99
A very tannic wine but with lovely sweet underlying fruit of obvious class – buy now but drink later, say in 2005. The Merlot grape ages very gracefully indeed and I can see this turning out to be a treat.

AUSTRALIA

7 **Dorrien Estate Bin 442 Shiraz 2001** £7.99
Relatively subtle for a Barossa Valley Shiraz, this has a minty-silky streak in the big upfront fruit.

7 **Lenbridge Forge Pinot Noir 2002** £8.99
Pale and interesting colour, an earthy-sweet Pinot with cherry background but serious length of flavour that certainly rivals village Burgundy for interest and value.

FRANCE

8 **Domaine de Dèves Côtes du Rhône 2001** £5.99
Good peppery rasp on the rim of the dense dark-fruit flavour in this well-made organic wine.

7 **Château de Surville Costières de Nîmes 2000** £6.99
Nice dense red from a high-flying appellation is somewhat extravagantly oaked.

8 **Château Planèzes 2000** £6.99
From France's deepest south, a big red of notable density with a dark, plummy-spicy middle flavour and nice edge of mint. Long aftertaste.

7 **Mercurey Domaine Levert 2001** £10.99
Burgundy, or to be more precise Chalonnais, of authentic character and actually reasonable value – slinky strawberry-raspberry Pinot Noir that even tastes expensive.

10 **Botteghino Chianti 2001** £5.99

Lush, black-cherry nose on this mature-tasting organically made Chianti, which has that delicious abrasion of acidity alongside the dense fruit that makes this such an ideal food wine. **BEST BUY**

8 **Chianti Superiore Burchino 2000** £5.99

Frightfully smart-looking ancient-map label on this young-tasting but lush and vanilla-laden Chianti, with bouncy raspberry fruit and classic nutskin, mouth-cleansing finish.

8 **Torre Scalza Montepulciano d'Abruzzo 2001** £6.99

From the Abruzzi hills on the Adriatic coast, a wine with beautiful colour like red velvet. But it's relatively light in body with a buzz of juicy fruit and quite an austere middle flavour. Lovely stuff but I think it will get even better if it lingers a year longer in bottle – so invest now, and be patient.

7 **Villa dei Furesi Primitivo di Puglia 2000** £6.99

A black sort of wine, very dense and dark in colour and with gripping blackberry fruit. A real meat-eater's red.

8 **Kaituna Hills Reserve Pinot Noir 2001** £9.99

Kiwi Pinot is brilliant but expensive and anything under a tenner might well be a bargain. A lovely summer-fruit wine with that distinctive Kiwi minty-glycerine kick in the flavour.

ITALY

NEW ZEALAND

PORTUGAL

8 **Quinta de Fafide Estate Reserva 2001**   £7.99
Port-scented, deep-purple, extravagant, oaked red from the Douro Valley (where the port comes from) – a special-occasion wine.

SPAIN

8 **Mantrana Rioja 2001**   £5.99
Colour already looks orange-rimmed with age and there's an inviting spice-and-cassis smell from a ripe, softly tannic and brightly fruity typical Rioja of evident quality.

7 **Navardia Rioja 2001**   £5.99
Yet another M&S Rioja, this time organic, it has lots of alcohol at 13.5 per cent and a blackcurrant-essence style bordering on the jammy – a big, purple, spearminty young wine for drinking now.

8 **Tomas Blanco Crespo Rioja 2001**   £6.99
Ripe, reserva style, with distinct vanilla on nose, this still has the clinging grip of tannin and could do with a bit longer in bottle.

8 **Campo Aldea Graciano Rioja 1996**   £7.99
Dense, limpid wine with lots of alcohol (13.5 per cent is high for Rioja) is nicely mature but retains its grip and has a good bite at the edge of the flavour.

URUGUAY

8 **Polo Sur Tannat 2000**   £9.99
Delicious dark brew from the obscure Tannat grape that has become Uruguay's speciality, this has a lush dark-chocolate centre to its big red fruitiness – lavish stuff.

USA

7 **Zamora Zinfandel 2001** £6.99
Sweet-briar nose in this squishy-fruit, easy-drinking middleweight sunny red, but beware – it is 15 per cent alcohol.

DRY WHITE WINES	UNDER £3

ITALY

10 **Bianco Beneventano 2002** £2.99
This is amazing for the money – a dry, crisp refresher from the Campania region (think of Naples) but with an underflavour that puts one in mind of the creamy egginess of carbonara sauce, and even a hint of smokiness at the finish. Just 11.5 per cent alcohol but it's no slouch. **BEST BUY**

DRY WHITE WINES	£3 TO £5

AUSTRALIA

8 **Pheasant Gully Bin 228**
Semillon-Sauvignon 2002 £4.99
Pure gooseberry on the nose, but this is quite a yielding wine – not too sharp with acidity – and noticeably fresh.

7 **Pheasant Gully Bin 492**
Gewürztraminer-Riesling 2002 £4.99
Interesting – the spice of the Gewürz is very evident and it has an exotic but dry style that captures something of Alsace – good with Asian food.

CHILE

7 **Casa Leona Chardonnay 2002** £4.99
Interesting brassica nose makes you think it might have Sauvignon in it, but it's pure Chardonnay and a decent one at that.

Domaine Mandeville Viognier
Vin de Pays d'Oc 2002 £3.99
Slightly syrupy smell on this perfectly good Languedoc Viognier, which is dry but reinforced with the grape's mysteriously unctuous character.

 Sauvignon Blanc Vin de Pays du Jardin
de la France 2002 £3.99
Nettles growing on a compost heap are most emphatically suggested in this stalwart Loire Valley Sauvignon – absolutely delicious wine for the money, no kidding.

 Muscadet Sèvre et Maine,
Le Moulin des Cossardières 2002 £4.99
Muscadet can be lean, eyewatering stuff but this one is gentle on the acidity and generous on the fruit with plenty of capacity to interest as well as to refresh.

 Pfalz Pinot Gris 2002 £4.99
Aromatic, faintly spritzy, delicately weighted (but 13 per cent alcohol) refreshingly floral Rhine wine of real character – in a claret-shaped bottle, presumably to disguise its German origin.

 Villa Masera Bianco Veronese 2002 £4.49
Organic wine from the Garganega grape of Soave fame is pleasingly pure and flavourful – understated but memorable.

 Villa Ulivi Pinot Grigio 2002 £4.99
Rather an austere variation of the endlessly trendy PG theme – good wine if you are averse to sweetness.

FRANCE

GERMANY

ITALY

Marks & Spencer

S AFRICA

8 **Rockridge Sauvignon Blanc 2002** £4.99
Good-value wine with nettles and asparagus on the nose and corresponding fruit, but with a less-assertive acidity than expected – easy drinking.

SPAIN

7 **Spanish White (1 litre)** £3.99
Very cheap – price is equal to £3 for a 75 cl bottle – this dry white from the Utiel Requena region has an interesting pear-blossom smell and enough freshness to justify its existence.

DRY WHITE WINES	OVER £5

ARGENTINA

8 **Tupungato Chardonnay 2001** £5.99
Gold in colour, it has suggestions of lanolin and beeswax on the nose and a rich, vanilla-toned, sweet-apple and peach fruitiness. Totally over the top, you might say – but great fun.

AUSTRALIA

8 **Banwell Farm Riesling 2002** £7.99
Classic Australian Riesling is stony-dry but forcefully flavoured with proper limey acidity – a great food wine.

8 **Lenbridge Forge Sauvignon Blanc 2002** £7.99
Aussie Sauvignons on the whole are not a patch on New Zealand's, but this asparagus-scented wine from the Yarra Valley in Victoria makes a good pitch. Quality wine with stacks of fruit and lovely, bright, lemon notes.

9 **Wickham Estate Chardonnay 1995** £11.00

A rarity – a really mature Aussie Chardy, this is the colour of a gold bar, and the label is covered in gold medals from the likes of the Cowra Wine Show and Melbourne Royal Wine Show. The nose is reminiscent of an over-the-hill Meursault but the flavour is intact, rich, creamy and evocative. A real fun wine for a special occasion and a lot cheaper than old Burgundy.

7 **Vouvray Domaine de la Pouvraie 2002** £5.50

Off-dry Loire wine from Chenin Blanc grapes has a honeyed scent and friendly soft melon-and-peach fruit – good aperitif.

7 **Oak Aged Bordeaux 2001** £6.99

I'm ashamed to admit this smelled to me more like Australian Chardonnay than the traditional Bordeaux-white mix of Sauvignon and Semillon, but it tastes more as expected – in fact rather luscious and classy.

7 **Chablis Domaine Pierre de Prehy 2001** £9.99

This is made by a famous producer, Jean-Marc Brocard, and is a nice gunflinty and well-flavoured example of the famous genre, but perhaps a shade expensive.

7 **St Romain, Nicolas Potel 2001** £9.99

Proper white Burgundy doesn't come cheap, and this is no exception, but it does have the classic qualities of the region's Chardonnay in its happy marriage of richness and briskness – an elegant wine.

8   **Pfalz Riesling 2002**   **£5.50**

With a ripe-apple nose and whiff of honey and a pleasing 'attack' of racy Riesling flavour on first sip, this is fine, limey-mineral dry wine of real character – in a claret-shape bottle.

8   **Darting Estate Dürkheimer Michelsberg Riesling 2002**   **£5.99**

Toffee-apple nose and altogether an apple pie of a wine – intense, structured, lively, long-flavoured.

8   **Georg Breuer Estate Riesling 2001**   **£7.99**

Note of spearmint in the brisk mineral aroma and matching brisk fruit.

8   **Pinot Grigio Podere, La Prendina Estate 2002**   **£5.99**

Exotic fruit-blossom nose and plenty of corresponding fruit with an interesting smoky backtaste.

8   **Torresoto White Rioja 2001**   **£5.99**

Grand gold colour and a nice, big, creamy, expensive nose on this rich and artfully poised dry white that would go very well with chicken or paella.

8   **Terra Douro Albariño 2002**   **£7.99**

From the Rias Baixas vineyards of Galicia, a very trendy region, this is a Sauvignon-like crisp refresher with extra richness and memorable character.

Marks & Spencer

NEW ZEALAND

10 **Kaituna Hills Reserve**
Sauvignon Blanc 2002 £7.99
This sings. Brisk, nettley perfume followed up by bags of
invigorating intense fruit with highlights like diamonds –
really exciting wine as good as any Kiwi brand I've tried.
BEST BUY

USA

8 **Freedom Ridge Viognier 2002** £5.99
Gold colour, lots of alcohol at 14 per cent and a
luxuriantly fruity dry white with all the Viognier's
characteristic apricotty, unctuous charms.

8 **Father Oak Chardonnay 2001** £7.99
Typical sunny Californian Chardonnay is lipsmackingly
ripe and seductive with lush highlights of warm peach
and melon.

SPARKLING WINES	OVER £5

FRANCE

8 **Champagne de St Gall 1998** £19.99
Alluring, biscuity whiff from this lively and dimensional
vintage fizz, which delivers a good depth of flavour for
the money.

Morrisons

Already the supermarket of choice to millions of shoppers in the North of England, Wakefield-based chain Morrisons has now entered the national consciousness by starting the bidding for Safeway.

It will no doubt be a long time before this takeover battle is resolved but Morrisons' bid plainly illustrates that this company, which has been run by the founder's son, Sir Ken Morrison, for the last 36 years, intends to go nationwide. Most of the 120 stores are north of Coventry – the furthest being at Tynemouth – but there are now branches in East London (Enfield and Chingford), Essex (Erith and Grays), Banbury in Oxfordshire, Letchworth in Hertfordshire, Cambourne in Cambridgeshire, Ipswich in Suffolk and several in South Wales. In 2004, the first branches will open in Scotland in Falkirk, Glasgow and Kilmarnock, and there is to be one in Bristol.

The wines have always enjoyed a following, and the list is indeed impressive, especially at under the all-important £5 mark. The company put on a huge tasting in London this year, the first I have ever been to, and it was illuminating.

Morrisons

ARGENTINA

 7 Slinky Shiraz 2002 £3.99

A Morrisons special, this has well-focused ripe red fruit. I must admit, I would approach a wine like this with more optimism if it did not have this annoying name. I didn't even think it did taste slinky.

**9 Prospect Hill Cabernet Sauvignon-
Petit Verdot 2000** £3.99

Seems very cheap for this rather poised, cedary-cassis, long-flavoured wine. It's almost claret-like, except that there's so much fruit it can only be New World.

AUSTRALIA

**7 Hardy's Bin 766
Cabernet Sauvignon 2002** £4.99

Safe, blackberry young red apparently made by Hardy's (now part of the world's biggest wine company, Constellation) for Morrisons.

7 Peter Lehmann Grenache 2001 £4.99

Rather pale orange-rimmed colour to this screwcap-bottle brand, but it has some good chewy fruit and isn't half as dried-out as it looks.

7 Woolpunda Cabernet Sauvignon 2000 £4.99

Big, obvious, upfront Cabernet with a pleasing completeness of flavour.

CHILE

8 Misiones Carmenère 2002 £4.99

This is a sweetie-pie of a wine – soft, plummy and beguiling in the true Carmenère style and a pretty good price too.

FRANCE

7 **Château Le Pin 2001** £3.99
Inky, Merlot-dominated, picnic Bordeaux with cheery charm. The name is the same as that of the region's most expensive wine, made across the river Gironde at Pomerol, which would set you back more than 50 times the price of this one.

8 **Fitou Mont Tauch 2001** £3.99
Very decent, darkly fruity, everyday wine from the Languedoc's most enterprising co-operative, Mont Tauch.

6 **Wild Pig Syrah Vin de Pays d'Oc 2001** £3.99
I know this is a very good seller, but however often I taste it I cannot get up any enthusiasm for it. Nice label and funny name, I suppose, but I find it rather boaring.

8 **Bourgogne Pinot Noir,
Cave de Lugny 2001** £4.29
Rather a pale colour, already going brown at the rim, but this light red Burgundy holds up well – lots of pleasant earthy-raspberry fruit for very little money.

8 **La Chasse du Pape, Gabriel Meffre 2001** £4.99
Ubiquitous Côtes du Rhône masquerading as Châteauneuf du Pape – dense and grippingly good with spice and warmth.

9 **Stephane & Philippe Cabernet Franc,
Maurel Vedeau 2000** £4.99
Vin de Pays d'Oc has the trademark 'leafy' scent and topnote of Cabernet Franc and beneath, a lush, sweetly-ripe, pure blackberry fruit – really very good indeed.

ITALY

7 **Montepulciano Uggiano 2001** £3.99
Great label on this, and the wine's not bad – very dark ruby-purple colour and attention-grabbing, zesty-brambly fruit.

8 **Brindisi DOC Rosso,
Cantina de Palma 2001** £4.49
Dark, coaly flavours of the Negroamaro grape centred on a likeable, sweetly ripe centre.

8 **Terranto Primitivo Puglia 2001** £4.79
Just about black in colour, a super-ripe wine from Italy's 'heel' that puts one in mind of blackcurrant soup – great stuff with sticky pasta dishes.

7 **Barbera d'Asti Balbi Soprani 2001** £4.99
Vigorous Piedmont red with purply-bright colour and flavour.

7 **Chianti Colli Fiorentini 2000** £4.99
A light style of Chianti – from the hills of Florence – but with lots of the characteristic cherry-raspberry fruit and relishable, clean, mouth-drying finish.

PORTUGAL

8 **Loios Red 2001** £4.49
'Sardine wine' it says in my note – by which I mean this is a typical red-fruit, minty, spicy Portuguese red that cries out for some typical Portuguese fare, but any exotic fishy dish will do.

SPAIN

🍷10 **M Red Rioja** £3.99
A humble, non-vintage, bog-standard Rioja, but it just happens to be utterly delicious – sweet vanilla-pod aroma over a positively artful strawberries-and-cream fruit.
BEST BUY

🍷8 **Montblanc 362
Tempranillo-Cabernet 2001** £3.99
From Conca de Barbera, a decent brambly glugger with a notable grip of flavour.

🍷7 **Poema Old Vine Garnacha,
Calatayud 2001** £4.99
Monster (14 per cent alcohol), black-fruit, super-ripe, near-raisiny eyebrow-raiser for meaty nights in.

USA

🍷8 **Seventh Moon Merlot 1999** £4.99
Alluring morello nose and ripe, round, richly mellow fruit in this sunny and heart-warming Californian – complete with groovy 1970s-type nomenclature.

RED WINES   OVER £5

AUSTRALIA

🍷5 **Lindemans Bin 45
Cabernet Sauvignon 2002** £5.99
This might be a famed and top-selling brand but it doesn't seem to be half the wine it used to be – appears to have gone downhill ever since they put the price up.

Morrisons

FRANCE

8 Château Caronne Ste Gemme 1997   £9.99
Well-known estate of the Haut Médoc in Bordeaux has made a nice wine in the 'light' 1997 vintage – middling weight but good tobacco-nose and slinky, quite intense, dark, ripe fruit. A posh bottle to take to a dinner party – with the considerable advantage that the wine is quite mature enough to drink now.

ITALY

7 Accademia del Sole Nero d'Avola-
Cabernet Sauvignon 2001   £5.99
Bit like a liqueur chocolate, this. There's a dark, tannic edge to the flavour, but inside it's all soft and ripe. Tastes a lot better than chocolate liqueur, of course.

7 Chianti Riserva Uggiano 1997   £7.49
Pricy but classy Chianti has rich vein of dark, sleek fruit that makes it an exciting glassful and classic clean finish.

S AFRICA

9 Tumara Pinotage 2001   £6.99
Pinotage – South Africa's own grape variety – is uniquely delicious but by no means in every case. This one is just right in its mix of plummy fragrance, smoothness and crunch. Tough one to describe, but it's bang on.

DRY WHITE WINES   £3 TO £5

AUSTRALIA

8 **Woolpunda Chardonnay 2001**   £4.45
Rather likeable, toffee-apple type of wine with plenty of
sunny fruit and a pleasantly slaking freshness.

8 **Peter Lehman Riesling 2001**   £4.99
Australian Rieslings are renowned for their limey-mineral
style and are utterly unlike their German counterparts.
But they are often rather expensive. This one's a bargain
with lots of fruit and at a price ideal if you're new to the
style and curious to try it out. Screwcap bottle.

7 **Yellow Tail Chardonnay 2002**   £4.99
Named after the yellowtail kangaroo and with apposite
designer label, this has tropical-peachy fruit and the
coconut background imparted by use of oak chips in the
fermenting tanks. It's jumping off the shelves in America,
where it is the biggest-selling of all imported wines, and
may well take off over here too.

8 **Yellow Tail Verdelho 2002**   £4.99
This flavoursome wine reminded me very much of pale,
bone-dry fino sherry, so if that's a style you like, you will
enjoy this Verdelho – a grape more usually associated
with the fortified wines of Madeira.

FRANCE

7 **Kiwi Cuvée Sauvignon Blanc 2001**   £3.99
A vin de pays of 'Le Jardin de la France' – the non-
appellation bit of the Loire Valley – this is made by a
New Zealander called Ben Jordaan who has failed
manfully to replicate the Sauvignons of his native country
but deserves two cheers for this zesty attempt.

Morrisons

FRANCE

🍷8 **Vouvray Pierre Guery 2001**   £4.49
This Chenin Blanc from the Loire is dry, but softly insinuating, and with traces of honey and cinnamon amidst the gently fresh fruit – scores high for interest.

🍷10 **Alsace Pinot Blanc Preiss Zimmer 2001**   £4.79
Perfect expression of the aromatic, herbaceous and fascinating Alsace style at a rarely affordable price – you couldn't find a better introduction to this undervalued region.   **BEST BUY**

🍷8 **Château St Galier Blanc Graves 2001**   £4.99
Classic, dry white Bordeaux has floral perfume, zippy but distinctly interesting, fresh mélange of fruit – pineapple, peach, hints of nectar – and elegant freshness.

🍷8 **Mâcon-Villages Jean-Pierre Teissedre 2000** £4.99
Interesting nuances of vanilla and white pepper in this mature southern Burgundy – it has tons of pleasing Chardonnay fruit with ripeness (13 per cent alcohol) and character. One of several encouragingly fresh and well-made Mâcon wines, at reasonable prices, I have come across this year.

GERMANY

🍷8 **Noble House Riesling, Ewald Pfeiffer 2001** £4.49
Rather an old-fashioned Moselle, grapey-sweet and soft, but still with the appley-racy rush of Riesling fruit keenly present – a very likeable aperitif wine.

S AFRICA

🍷7 **Hill and Dale Sauvignon Blanc 2002**   £4.99
Good attempt at a style so dominated by New Zealand, this is a zingy nettley Sauvignon of more than passable freshness and interest. Cape Sauvignon Blanc, with its consistent price advantage over the Kiwi version, is a wine style with a great future.

SPAIN

🍷7 **Montblanc 362 Viura-Chardonnay 2002**   £3.99
Viura is the grape from which creamy white Rioja is made, and in this combination with Chardonnay it makes what might be described as a freshened-up version of the Rioja – quite fun.

🍷8 **Poema Sauvignon Blanc Rueda 2002**   £4.99
Nice, fizzingly brisk aroma from this fresh and flowery Sauvignon with a crisp finish. From Spain's Rueda region, a centre of excellence for wines of this rather un-Spanish style.

🍷7 **Terramar Chardonnay de Muller,
Tarragona 2001**   £4.99
This is called a white wine but has a distinct pink-orange tint to match its intriguing gamey-ripe flavour – altogether rather mysterious, but a nice interesting glassful.

USA

🍷7 **Ironstone Obsession 2001**   £4.99
Made from a grape called Symphony, this is a bit of curiosity – muscatty dry white with ripeness and delicacy.

🍷7 **Seventh Moon Chardonnay 2001**   £4.99
Nice bit of caramel toffee in this straightforward Californian varietal.

DRY WHITE WINES   **OVER £5**

FRANCE

🍷7 **Alsace Gewürztraminer Preiss
Zimmer 2001**   £5.99
Rather a sweet Gewürz but still pleasingly typical with its lychee smell and exotic spicy fruit.

Morrisons

FRANCE

7 **Sirius Bordeaux Blanc 2001** £5.99
Big-brand, dry white that has real intensity of fruit – not the 'flabby' wetness one fears in commercial Bordeaux whites – and is bravely bone-dry. Serious, classy wine, if a little expensive.

GERMANY

8 **Pfeiffer Riesling Spätlese 2001** £6.99
Splendid gaudy label on this palpably ripe yet deliciously mineral Moselle with a nifty balance between grapiness and citrus acidity.

7 **Zeltinger Sonnenuhr Auslese 2001** £7.99
Ripe, but by no means sweet, young Moselle with evident traces of raisiny concentration – not for keeping, though.

ITALY

7 **Accademia del Sole**
Catarratto-Viognier 2001 £5.99
Plenty of assertive peachy flavour in this big wine with a trace of butterscotch and a pleasant dry finish.

NEW ZEALAND

8 **Moa Ridge Sauvignon Blanc 2002** £5.99
Powerful asparagus smell and bristling, bright, briny fruit in this bargain Kiwi Sauvignon – keen flavours and keen price.

Safeway

The people who work at Safeway cannot be having an easy time of it. With several bidders in the ring for a chain the press is perpetually describing as 'ailing' or 'under-performing', staff are constantly reminded that they face a future in which some new owner or another will shut half the stores or 'rebrand' them all. In a bizarre opinion poll conducted among Safeway customers in the summer of 2003, only 15 per cent of a thousand people questioned said they cared whether Safeway survived or not, and many said they thought it would be a good thing if the chain was taken over by Asda.

Given this grim prospect, the Safeway stores I visit from time to time seem creditably cheerful places. And in the midst of all the takeover talk, many branches have transformed their drinks departments into very smart enclaves, where it is rather more of a pleasure to browse than before.

The wines are looking as good as ever, with plenty of choice, reasonable prices and regular discounts offered right across the range. You'll always get a five per cent discount if you buy six or more bottles of wine.

Safeway

RED WINES	UNDER £3

SPAIN

🍷8 **Don Coyote Red**   £2.69

The name on this screwcap plonk from Valencia always makes me smile, and the wine itself doesn't make me all that unhappy either. A student-friendly red that is neither too sweet nor too rough and would be a wily choice for the likes of sangria.

RED WINES	£3 TO £5

AUSTRALIA

🍷7 **Jindalee Shiraz 2002**   £4.99

The interest here is in the nice crisp 'entry' to the flavour – a standard big, soft Shiraz with an edge to the fruit that impresses.

FRANCE

🍷8 **Côtes du Roussillon Villages 2000**   £4.09

Delicious, own-label, warm, dark and pepper-centred soft red from an AC not so much seen in the supermarkets these days – delicious winter drinking with hearty stews.

🍷8 **Bourgueil Les Chevaliers 2001**   £4.99

Elusive Loire appellation of Bourgueil makes some of the region's best reds from Cabernet Franc grapes and this is one to seek out – firm, healthy fruit and a distinctive style.

🍷2 **French Revolution**
     Syrah & Grenache 2002   £4.99

This widely available brand is a disgrace. It is lean, stalky, mean and sour. Has the buyer at Safeway – or in any of the other supermarkets stocking this wine – actually tasted it? It would be a bad buy even at £2.99 and needs to be avoided.

7 La Nature Nero d'Avola 2001 £4.49
Organic, dark and earthy red from Sicily is good with pasta, but I wish they wouldn't use organic corks – the first bottle I bought was ruined by TCA and I had to take it back.

7 Volcanica Aglianco 2001 £4.99
From the Basilicata region, this is an intriguing middleweight, thoroughly Italian red, firmly fruity with likeable earthy, dry style.

8 Tinto da Anfora 1999 £4.99
This hardy perennial from the Alentejo region has comes down in price (in Safeway, at least) and deserves trying for its minty, black-fruit ripeness and maturity. The maker reckons it can be kept ten years to develop, but I wouldn't leave it that long.

10 Maximo Tempranillo 2000 £3.99
This is a mere Tempranillo Tinto of the vague designation Vino de la Tierra de Castillo, but it has super, keen-edged, raspberry fruitiness with obvious but manageable oaky vanillin – lush, lively and thoroughly Spanish, even down to the patriotic label and matching cork. **BEST BUY**

8 Vino d'Arte Bierzo 2001 £3.99
From the mysterious Mencia grape grown in the obscure Bierzo region, a pleasingly sunny, fleshy, soft and typically Spanish red glugger.

7 Siglio 1881 Rioja 2001 £4.99
Straightforward, middleweight, vanilla-toned wine in recognisable style.

Safeway

ARGENTINA

8 Norton Barrel Select Malbec 2000   £6.99
Notably dense and dark colour to this meaty red with a bitter-chocolate centre and yet an undaunting weight – a pleasing wine.

7 Bodega Norton Privada 2000   £9.99
I've been following this wine for years. It's made in Mendoza from a typical Bordeaux mix of Cabernet, Merlot and Malbec, and used to taste like a sort of super-sunny Médoc, with mountains of fruit but an elegant restraint. Now it's rather more upfront, but still a very enjoyable luxury wine.

FRANCE

8 Beaujolais Villages Combes aux Jacques Louis Jadot 2001   £6.29
This score is conditional – I'm assuming that Safeway has got the 2001 vintage in by the time you are reading this. If it still has the 1999 or 2000 (which it did at time of writing), give it a miss. But if you're curious to know what good Beaujolais is really like, try this deliciously bouncy, juicy and refreshing red from one of Burgundy's great trading companies, Louis Jadot, which has made a great wine in 2001. Note, though, price is lower elsewhere.

8 Calvet Bordeaux Réserve 2000   £6.49
From the successful millennium vintage, this is a warmly ripe, mature-tasting claret with proper cedary character – and a lot more satisfying ripe fruit than is (sadly) usual in generic Bordeaux these days. This excellent wine from one of Bordeaux's biggest negociant firms is frequently discounted, so look out for it while the 2000 vintage lasts.

FRANCE

8 **Vinsobres Côtes du Rhône Villages,**
Perrin 2000 £6.99
This smartly presented village wine by the Perrin family
– makers of very grand Châteauneuf – is darkly spicy,
powerful and complex. Best decanted.

ITALY

8 **Langhe Nebbiolo, Araldica 1999** £6.99
Nebbiolo is the grape that makes Barolo, Italy's grandest
wine, and this is a fair imitation of the style – from fruit
grown in the Langhe hills of Piedmont, close to the
Barolo denomination. It has a pale-ish, bricky colour,
enticingly scented of roses, manageably tannic and
crammed with black-cherry and almond flavours –
fascinating stuff. The first bottle I bought was horribly
corky but the replacement was fine.

DRY WHITE WINES £3 TO £5

ITALY

8 **Verdicchio dei Castelli di Jesi,**
Castellani 2001 £3.99
Thoroughly refreshing and gently spicy dry white in the
trademark 'amphora' shape bottle is a good buy.

SOUTH AFRICA

8 **Danie de Wet Chardonnay 2002** £4.49
Can't resist this perfect name for a winemaker, and this
everyday fresh, bright and well-extracted Chardonnay is
pretty irresistible too at the price. You may notice it's
labelled 'sur Lie', French for 'on the lees', which means
the wine has been left in contact with the yeasty detritus
of its fermentation in the vat for a while, to pick up extra
flavours.

AUSTRALIA

7 Rosemount Estate Diamond Riesling 2002 £6.99
From one of the coolest Australian vintages in decades, a well-coloured, richly perfumed Riesling with a nice whiff of rose petals and a big, tastebud-grabbing, lime-finishing, crisp fruitiness with 13.5 per cent alcohol – all in a screwcap bottle.

ITALY

8 I Portali Greco Basilicata 2001   £5.49
The white Greco grape has Greek origins (obvious enough from the name) and makes a well-coloured, aromatic and refreshingly dry white with notes of pineapple and herbs all trimmed up with a clean, limey finish.

8 Soave Classico Superiore Pra 2001   £6.99
Delicious, stony-fresh, aromatic example of the Soave style – positively elegant in its balance of sleek fruit and gently citric acidity.

NEW ZEALAND

**9 Montana Unoaked East Coast
Chardonnay 2002   £5.99**
This is a glittering wine, lemon-gold in colour and with a matching citrussy background to the lively, pineapple fruit. It echoes the unique fresh-yet-intense style that so marks out New Zealand's great Sauvignon wines, and as such is another happy variation on this ever-extending theme.

8 Oyster Bay Sauvignon Blanc 2002   £6.99
Zesty yet well-concentrated Kiwi classic from the lower reaches of what can sometimes seem a rather steeply ascending price scale.

USA

8 **Ironstone Vineyards Chardonnay 2000** £5.99
Dramatic yellow colour and alluring sweet-apple nose
packs a lot of generous fruit into a wine that more than
matches Aussie brands at this price for interest and value
– give it a try.

8 **Bonterra Chardonnay 1999** £8.49
Pretty expensive, but this organic Californian is a riot of
lavish, pure and mineral flavours that lingers long in the
memory and is outstanding by any measure.

SWEET WHITE WINES	OVER £5

FRANCE

10 **La Fleur d'Or 1999 (half bottle)** £5.99
This is a great treat, a good-quality Sauternes at an
unusually reasonable price even for a half bottle – pure-
gold colour, intoxicatingly honeyed 'noble rot' nose, and
sumptuous, sunburnt, honeyed fruit complete with
correcting acidity at the finish. **BEST BUY**

────── J Sainsbury ──────

Sainsbury's might trail in the wake of Tesco when it comes to sheer size and turnover, but it is in no way lagging behind in the wine department. The range is huge, and although packed out with the usual proliferation of Australian and Californian mega-brands, there are plenty of interesting individual wines squeezed in between.

You need to take your time in Sainsbury's because it has particular strengths. This year the Loire Valley is especially well represented. So is the Rhône, but stock up from this region's 2000 and 2001 vintages, because 2002 was a wash-out. I don't think much of Sainsbury's French 'country' wines – those from outside the classic regions – but it does have a good choice of reds from Spain. Australia seems utterly dominated by the universal brands, but there are some interesting, less well-known wines among the New Zealand and South African lists.

Sainsbury's seem to be going upmarket. There are more estate clarets and Burgundies, reserve Riojas and Chiantis than I can remember before. At the most recent tasting, it put on a number of extravagantly expensive wines from its two London 'flagship' stores, the Cromwell Road branch and the newly opened Sainsbury's Market at Bluebird, Terence Conran's emporium in the King's Road. Just for fun, I have included my notes on some of these wines, which were priced up to £100 and above.

8 **Sainsbury's Argentinian Red** £2.99

Decent, anonymous, jug dry red tastes healthy and ripe – can't fault it. This is a non-vintage wine, blended from the harvests of two or more years, and does have a pleasing note of maturity.

9 **Sainsbury's Argentinian Bonarda 2002** £3.99

On supermarket own-label Argentinian wines I always sneak a look at the back label and if I find the name Zuccardi or La Agricola or Santa Julia, I take heart. Those names are of the family, vineyards and brand, respectively, of the country's equal-best (with Nicolas Catena) big-scale wine producer. This one is a Zuccardi – with nice, big, brambly nose, vigorous fruit with chocolate centre, and a reassuring completeness. Somehow rather Italian in style, and delicious.

8 **Lo Tengo Malbec 2002** £4.99

This has a gimmicky label incorporating a hologram of a tango being danced but in spite of that it is a very decent wine with soft, mocha-hinting, dark fruit that will make a good partner, as they say, for salsa dishes.

8 **Jindalee Cabernet Sauvignon 2002** £4.99

Popular brand has jolly dark, glyceriney, eucalyptus fruit with a character of its own. Anything from Australia at under £5 with a bit of character is worth trying and this is no exception.

Sainsbury

CHILE

7 **Casillero del Diablo Cabernet Sauvignon 2001** £4.99

Workmanlike Cabernet has Chilean ripeness and tidy, blackcurrant style.

8 **Casillero del Diablo Carmenère 2001** £4.99

Easy-drinking, dry, leafy red with clean edginess has an Italianate charm that will make it a good match with fish. Made by the venerable Concha y Toro. Beware, though, that while there is a good Cabernet Sauvignon under this label, there is also a Malbec, which tastes diabolical.

FRANCE

8 **La Chasse du Pape, Gabriel Meffre 2001** £4.99

Ubiquitous Côtes du Rhône masquerading as Châteauneuf du Pape – dense and grippingly good with spice and warmth.

SPAIN

7 **Santerra Tempranillo 2001** £3.99

Raisiny whiff to this commercial brand from the Utiel Requena region belies the pleasant juicy bright fruitiness on the palate – a decent middleweight food wine.

RED WINES OVER £5

ARGENTINA

9 **Sainsbury's Reserve Selection Malbec 2002** £5.49

Deliciously approachable, blackberry-fruit, smooth red with poised ripeness and purity from the Malbec grape, which the Argentines are fast turning into a cult.

8 **Norton Barrel Select Malbec 2000** £6.99

Notably dense and dark colour to this meaty red with a bitter-chocolate centre and yet an undaunting weight – a pleasing wine.

ARGENTINA

7 **Canale Black River Reserve Malbec 2001** £8.99
Appropriately black colour and a vanilla-laden, oaky nose on this velvety monster (14.5 per cent alcohol) from Patagonia.

AUSTRALIA

8 **Sainsbury's Reserve Selection**
Australian Shiraz 2001 £5.03
Strong, spicy Shiraz with concentration but innocent of overripeness (though note 14 per cent alcohol) and dangerously easy to drink. Rather better than big-brand Shirazes like Lindemans, which cost £1 more.

7 **Henschke Hill of Grace Shiraz 1997** £95.00
On an objective basis I have to score this with a mere 7, but if it had a realistic price of, say, under £30, I'd give it 10. It has the liveliest possible perfume of heavenly fruit and an ineffable density, a sort of unbearable lightness of being. Okay, it can't really be sensibly described but is a quite beautiful wine and if you are very rich, buy a bottle. It's on sale only at Sainsbury's 'Bluebird' store in King's Road, London SW3, or you can buy lots of different incredible Henschke wines from merchant Lay & Wheeler of Colchester, Essex (01206 764446).

CHILE

8 **Sainsbury's Reserve Selection**
Chilean Merlot 2001 £5.79
Friendly morello-cherry fruit with depth and length in this satisfying, pure-fruit middleweight.

7 **Errazuriz Estate Syrah 2001** £6.99
Silk and spice in this smooth crowd-pleaser.

7 **Mont Gras Carmenère Reserva 2001** £6.99
Generous if rather obviously oaked smoothie.

CHILE

🍷7 **Marques de Casa Concha Merlot 2001**   £7.99
Damson fruit as well as classic morello cherry notes in this very dark, intense, massively ripe (14 per cent alcohol) item.

🍷9 **Domaine de la Grande Bellane 1999**   £6.03
This màture Côtes du Rhône Villages is a snip at this price, from a great vintage that must surely by now be in very short supply. Snap it up for its intense, spicy, exhilaratingly developed flavours of the far south. Organic.

🍷8 **Château de la Garde 1999**   £6.99
Claret from the humble Bordeaux Supérieur appellation, but smartly presented and in the ripe, approachably rounded, sleek-blackcurrant style now becoming more evident among the region's generic wines. Recommended.

FRANCE

🍷7 **La Chasse du Pape Grande Réserve 2001**   £6.99
I thought this was the ubiquitous Chasse du Pape brand – a Châteauneuf-du-Pape pretender – at a hugely inflated price until I discovered it is a grand reserve variation on the original successful formula. It's a darker, more tannic and spicy edition and worth trying if you don't begrudge the extra £2.

🍷8 **Sainsbury's Classic Selection
St Emilion 2000**   £9.99
Yes, it's expensive for a supermarket own-label, but this is a genuinely beguiling, mature, silky claret from a good vintage – as good as anything you'd get at this price with a pretty picture of a château on it.

🍷6 **Sainsbury's Classic Selection
Margaux 2000**   £12.99
Lovely inviting violets and briar nose but the fruit doesn't warrant the price.

8 **Château Cantemerle 1997** £13.99

A rare thing in a supermarket, this 'classed growth' claret is sweetly ripe and appealing in spite of being from a despised vintage. Actually it's rather good, and the château's name has a nice story behind it. During the 100 Years War, a mob of occupying English troops encamped at the old castle and set about looting the wine. In the grounds stood a huge, sooty cannon affectionately known as the *merle* – blackbird – and the estate workers hauled it up to the cellar doors, lit the fuse, and retired to a safe distance. The subsequent stupendous explosion terrified the unwelcome guests off the property, which was then renamed *cante merle* – the blackbird's song.

10 **Réserve de la Comtesse 1997** £17.99

Among all Sainsbury's posh French reds, this is the one to go for. It's the 'second' wine of top 'classed growth' estate Château Pichon Lalande, meaning it's made from the less mature vines and vats rejected for the grand vin (costing fifty quid a bottle) itself. But even in the very ordinary 1997 vintage this has turned out to be a real classic – lovely, cedary, supple, mature, special-occasion claret for the same price as, say, indifferent champagne.

BEST BUY

7 **Château de Beaucastel,**
Châteauneuf du Pape 1997 £24.99

This wine is on sale in Sainsbury's 25 biggest megastores only and I include it just for interest, given the price. Beaucastel is rated by some experts to be the best estate of Châteauneuf. In the 1997 vintage – not a great one – the wine is rather lean, though showing traces of the glorious rich complexities of the appellation, and it may develop with a few more years in the bottle. Or it may not.

FRANCE

Sainsbury

FRANCE

6 **Château Cheval Blanc 1996** £139.99

Yes, the price is not a misprint. This is one of the great *crus classés* of Bordeaux, sold only in Sainsbury's 'Bluebird' branch in King's Road, London SW3, and having tasted it, I feel duty-bound to describe it. Although from a recent, but good, vintage, the colour is already going disinctly orange at the rim; it has an inviting 'cigar-box' nose and is already rounded-out enough to drink with pleasure – at someone else's expense, presumably.

ITALY

8 **Inycon Aglianico 2001** £5.03

This is one of the better wines in the Inycon range from Sicily. It's a big meaty red with 13.5 per cent alcohol and starts a bit raisiny, but in the glass it quickly blooms into a fleshy, earthy and relishable food matcher – pizza, for once, comes to mind.

7 **Inycon Shiraz 2002** £5.03

I have mixed feelings about these ubiquitous Inycon wines from Sicily's giant Serrestori co-operative. This one has a very bright purple colour, a distinct elderberry style, and seems rather jammy, but I quite like it in a country-wine sort of way. As ever – it's very sunny in Sicily – there's a lot of alcohol, at 14 per cent.

7 **Jamie Oliver Montepulciano**
d'Abruzzo 2001 £5.03

Nice, typical brambly wine described by the celebrity chef as 'so chocolatey and gamey and smooth' – giving us punters the chance to compare notes and determine whether we have celebrity taste or not.

9 Valpolicella Capitel dei Nicalo, Tedeschi 1999 £6.99

A grand classico superiore Valpolicella with classic cherry-and-almonds style and softly gripping middleweight fruit with length and dimension. The sort of wine that gives now-unfashionable Valpolicella back some of its good name.

8 Amativo 2000 £7.99

From Salento in the far south, a dark, roasted sort of intense, earthy red of a thoroughly Italian kind with a whopping 14.5 per cent alcohol – fab with a complicated baked pasta dish.

4 Tignanello 1999 £44.99

A 'super-Tuscan' that tastes a lot like a rather young but quite decent riserva Chianti. At a blind tasting, I would price it around £9.

3 Conterno Fantino Barolo Vigna del Gris 1998 £49.99

Orange-brown colour at the rim and a fetching sweet, nutty nose on this splendid wine from Italy grandest denomination, Barolo in Piedmont. But the tannins are still masking the fruit – and will, I believe, outlast it.

8 Mount Difficulty Pinot Noir 2001 £16.99

Kiwi Pinot Noirs are wonderful, but never cheap. In the scheme of things, this oddly named example is pretty fair value for a divinely slinky, minty, summer-fruit classic of positively cerebral complexity.

J Sainsbury

PORTUGAL

9   **Grand'Arte Touriga Franca 2001**   £7.03
Terrific, minty-sweet core to this rather porty heavyweight (14.5 per cent alcohol), which contrives to balance clean dryness of style with a velvety opulence that would do equal justice to a grand roast or a chunk of Stilton.

SOUTH AFRICA

9   **Goats do Roam 2002**   £5.03
Terrific, deliciously yielding, but robust, firm and ripe bargain red is made largely from South Africa's indigenous grape variety, the Pinotage. The odd name is a tilt at French Côtes du Rhône but also celebrates the fact that the maker, Charles Back, is a goat farmer as well. A herd of 600 of them roam his Fairview estate, and some of South Africa's best cheese is made from their milk.

8   **Sainsbury's Reserve Selection**
       South African Shiraz 2001   £5.49
Friendly grip to this brambly, purple-black red with plumpness and length of flavour – a likeable wine at this price.

7   **Carneby Liggle Old Bush Vine Red 2002**   £6.03
Curious brûlé aroma from this big butch red – probably just the thing to drink with biltong.

SPAIN

8   **Conde de Siruela 2000**   £5.03
Intensely ripe and minty red from the highly rated Ribera del Duero region has the depth and darkness of fruit to stand up to strong-flavoured dishes.

8 **Vega Sicilia Valbuena 1996**   **£54.99**

This is from the Ribera del Duero region and belongs to an esoteric range of red wines reckoned to be the best – and certainly the most expensive – of Spain. This one has dense ruby colour, a huge, minty, classic cassis Cabernet Sauvignon aroma and masses of dark, silky fruit. It's a wine of obvious merit and while the price seems ridiculous, it's cheap by the standards of, say, upper-echelon Bordeaux. I love the naff farmhouse-jam-type label.

SPAIN

ROSÉ WINES	£3 TO £5

8 **Santa Julia Syrah Rosé 2003**   **£4.99**

Hearty, magenta-coloured, dry wine has a bramble-and-spice fruitiness, lots of ripeness (13.5 per cent alcohol) and will be much at its best with food – just about any food you care to mention, which is one of the attractions of rosé.

ARGENTINA

7 **Cuvée Victoria Rosé de Provence 2002**   **£5.49**

Smoked-salmon colour to this quite dry but flavoursome (raspberry dominates) and fresh vin gris from the South of France in a fun bottle with a picturesque label.

FRANCE

7 **Agramont Garnacha Rosado 2002**   **£4.03**

Startling shocking-pink colour to this wine from Navarra and a flavour that is pure strawberries – good, innocent glugger, though beware the 13 per cent alcohol.

SPAIN

AUSTRALIA

7 Jindalee Chardonnay 2002 £4.99
Hint of well-buttered scrambled egg in this strong-flavoured, 14-per-cent-alcohol heavyweight at a fair price. 'Jindalee' rather boringly means 'bare hill' in Aborigine.

FRANCE

8 Lurton Chenin Blanc 2002 £3.99
A VdP of the Jardin de la France – a picturesque way of saying the Loire – this fresh, dry white with just 11 per cent alcohol has a nice spring-blossom smell and lots of tangy fruit, more lemony than usually associated with the soft style of the Chenin Blanc grape. In fact, it's a grassy, assertive wine you might easily mistake for a Sauvignon.

10 Atlantique Sauvignon Blanc 2002 £4.99
From the Loire's Atlantic estuary, this wine fully lives up to its maritime name with an aroma that is pure sea breeze. Perfect wine to go in and with the moules marinières, and a harbinger of summer with its lemony zest and sunny fruit. **BEST BUY**

8 Calvet Limited Release
Sauvignon Blanc 2002 £4.99
Calvet is a big commercial producer in Bordeaux, and for once big is beautiful. This is a generous, tangy, grassy-lemony Sauvignon that really gets hold of the tastebuds.

8 La Couronne des Plantagenets 2001 £4.99
Lush Vouvray has a spring-blossom whiff and bright, fresh fruit in which honey lingers deliciously in the background. This is good on its own, but also drinks very well with chicken or creamy pasta dishes.

FRANCE

7 **Sainsbury's Classic Selection Muscadet**
Sèvre et Maine, Jean Douillard 2002 £4.99
Plenty of zing on the nose, it's positively uplifting. This is a big mouthful, quite challenging with overt acidity – but just short of fierce. Muscadet with muscle.

GERMANY

7 **St Alban Spätlese 2001** £3.83
Lemon-gold in colour, perfumed with honey and apple blossom, and softly ripe – perfect for drinking well-chilled in the garden and only a modest 9 per cent alcohol.

8 **Kendermanns Pinot Grigio 2002** £4.03
In Germany, the grape the Italians call Pinot Grigio is usually known as the Rülander, but who would buy wine called Rülander? So the enterprising people at Kendermanns have cheekily adopted the Italian style – and have made a wine with a lot more tang and smokiness than plenty of the sub-Alpine versions I have tried. Highly recommended dry wine.

ITALY

9 **Jamie Oliver Val de Molini**
Garganega di Verona 2001 £4.03
In spite of, not because of, its endorsement by Sainsbury's nakedly loyal celebrity chef, this gets very high marks because it is a brilliant dry white, crisp but lush, fresh but intensely fruity, and with appreciable depth of flavour. Jamie declares on the label he '…thought Garganega was an Italian sausage until I tasted this wine'.

9   **Argento Chardonnay 2002**   £5.03

This is a well-known brand from Nicolas Catena that delivers more flavour and interest than just about any other Chardonnay I can think of at the price – lush, peachy stuff but with a pure, bright fruitiness that brings a smile. It's a safe bet and seems to be on sale just about everywhere.

7   **Argento Chardonnay Reserva 2001**   £6.99

Argento's standard Chardonnay is one of my top-value wines this year, and this oak-aged reserve version at £2 more is no slouch either with its creamy-almondy style and assertive ripe, appley, bright fruit – good special-occasion wine.

10   **Catena Agrelo Vineyards Chardonnay 2001**   £9.99

Nicholas Catena – who also makes Argento wines (see above) has achieved iconic status for the Chardonnay that bears his name. It is amazingly consistent year after year, and the price has risen only modestly. This is a chance to taste the apogee of Argentine Chardonnay – rich, pure, mineral wine of memorable character.
BEST BUY

8   **Canepa Winemaker's Selection Gewürztraminer 2002**   £5.03

Spice and lychee come through clearly on the nose of this perennial Alsace-style, dry but exotic wine – which this year is drier than usual, making it, I would say, an improvement (too many Alsace Gewürzes are over-sweet), – a more exciting glassful even than before.

ARGENTINA

CHILE

FRANCE

8 Sainsbury's Classic Selection
Vouvray 2002   £5.99

Nice nectary note in the middle and finish of this dry Chenin Blanc from the Loire appellation of Vouvray gives it above-average interest. Good as an aperitif wine as well as with antipasto, salad and chicken dishes.

7 Sainsbury's Classic Selection
Pouilly Fumé 2002   £8.99

Nice bit of colour, and an inviting, complex nose on this Loire Sauvignon from the appellation next-door to Sancerre. It's a fresh, structured wine with hints of woodsap – but no smoke – and assertive fruit all along its length. Worth the money.

7 Domaine du Château du Meursault 1999 £19.99

Lavish white Burgundy from a famed estate owned by industrial-scale negociant Patriarche has rich gold colour but in spite of its relative maturity is still tasting a shade green. It's a great wine for show, but you can do a lot better for this kind of money.

GERMANY

8 Dr Loosen Riesling 2002   £5.99

On the surface of it, a humble QbA wine, but there is bumper fruit in this crackingly ripe and racy Moselle from the formidable Ernie Loosen, with 8.5 per cent alcohol and zingy, lingering fruit.

GERMANY

🍷10 **Villa Wolf Pinot Gris 2001** £5.99

This is an amazing wine, made in the Rheinpfalz or 'Palatinate' region from the grape usually known as the Rülander in Germany, but here going under its French name and in an extravagant Burgundy-style bottle. The wine is gold in colour with a nose suggesting vanilla and a lavish, rich-but-fresh style with 13.5 per cent alcohol – extraordinary, delicious stuff, made by one of Germany's star winemakers, Ernie Loosen, and cheap for what it is.
BEST BUY

🍷7 **Dr Loosen Graacher Himmelreich Riesling Kabinett 2002** £8.99

Pale Moselle has a crisp-apple nose but a great impact of sweet-apple fruit in the mouth and lots of length – classic Riesling with just 7.5 per cent alcohol and potentially long life if you have the patience.

ITALY

🍷7 **Inycon Fiano 2002** £5.03

Fiano is a revival of a wine known to the ancient Romans, and this Sicilian rendering under the well-known Inycon brand has a distinctly Old-World feel to it – yellow colour, a nutty rather oxidised, dry style reminiscent of old-fashioned white Rioja. Interesting wine to try with strong cheese.

NEW ZEALAND

🍷7 **Sanctuary Sauvignon Blanc 2002** £6.03

Very asparagussy, crisp, dry white with grassy freshness and lots of length – all at a price that is distinctly modest on the Kiwi scale.

🍷7 **Nobilo Sauvignon Blanc 2002** £7.03

A mélange of gooseberry and asparagus flavours with textbook crispness, this is a contemplative Kiwi dry white that scores highly for structured interest.

NEW ZEALAND

🍷8   **Villa Maria Riesling 2002**   £7.03

Lashings of limey fruit in this well-made Kiwi food-wine (for chicken and heartier fish dishes among others). Mineral, lively and lingering – and in a radically chic screwcap bottle.

🍷7   **Villa Maria Sauvignon Blanc 2002**   £8.03

The Marlborough estate of Villa Maria makes one of the world's great Sauvignons. In this vintage, asparagus is very much to the fore on the nose and in the fruit – right through. A huge, ripe (13 per cent alcohol) stand-alone or fish-matching wine worth the money. Screwcap bottle.

SOUTH AFRICA

🍷7   **Graham Beck Chardonnay 2002**   £5.99

Sweet toffee nose on this old-fashioned, extra-ripe (14 per cent alcohol) dry white with plenty of style – and ample bright fruit, not masked by the fact that it has been fermented in oak.

🍷8   **Springfield Estate Special Cuvée Sauvignon Blanc 2002**   £6.99

Sweet blossom nose on this fully developed Cape Sauvignon but plenty of lemony zest too – a proper competitor with its Kiwi counterparts for value and interest.

SPAIN

🍷8   **Sainsbury's Classic Selection Albariño 2001** £7.03

Albariño is the trendiest white grape in Spain these days, known for its creamy but zesty style, especially when grown in the Rias Baixas region, which this wine comes from. This is a delicious, herbaceous, dry white with fathoms of flavour – Spain's answer, I'd call it, to top-quality New Zealand Sauvignon Blanc.

USA

 7   **Gallo Coastal Vineyards**
Chardonnay 2000   **£9.99**
From California's – in fact the world's – biggest winery, this theatrically rich (14 per cent alcohol), new-oak dry white contrives to be impressively light on its feet. Gallo is a global brand, but this top-of-the-range wine shows they can do special things as well.

SWEET WHITE WINES	OVER £5

 8   **Domaine Léonce Cuisset 2001 (50 cl)**   **£6.99**
From the Saussignac AC near Bergerac, a weighty sweet white from Semillon grapes has honey heart, terrific density, but poised acidity – a voluptuous wine in the style of Monbazillac.

FRANCE

8   **Sainsbury's Classic Selection**
Sauternes 2001 (half bottle)   **£8.99**
Ambrosia! Mind you, it needs to be at this price. Gorgeous gold colour and a pure 'botrytis' nose on a honeyed fruit-basket of a wine with perfect acidity that aspires to the quality of even more expensive names – a great treat to sip with blue cheese or dates rather than with puddings, which will mask the nuances.

Somerfield

Angela Mount is one of the big players in the British wine trade. As wine buyer for Somerfield, she is responsible for filling the shelves of more than 1,300 stores – including the Kwik Save chain – in which 13 million people throughout Britain shop every week.

An Oxford languages graduate with a commanding intelligence, she is at home in the role of the big-company executive, but what seems really to excite her most about her job is the down-to-earth business of seeking out the very best wines she can afford within the tough budgets imposed in the fiercely competitive world of supermarket retailing.

Angela has been at the Bristol-based company for ten years, starting just as the former 'Gateway' stores began to transmogrify into the Somerfield chain of today. And in that relatively short time she has built a range of wines that competes convincingly with those of the 'Big Four' supermarkets.

But it's something of a Cinderella operation. With a turnover of a mere £5 billion a year, Somerfield is a relatively small retailer compared to the giants. The company is constantly the target of takeover rumours. But the wines, especially the own-label range – accounting for about 150 of the 500 different wines they sell and entirely created by Angela Mount – are in many cases the equal of those of bigger rivals. 'I want them to be the best in the business,' says Angela, 'and to be the best they have to be very good indeed.'

RED WINES   £3 TO £5

Somerfield

ARGENTINA

9 **Somerfield Argentine Sangiovese 2002** £3.99
Particularly soft and squishy style from the Chianti
grape, made by top producer La Agricola, delivers
summer flavours in abundance – great pasta-matcher.

10 **Somerfield Argentine Tempranillo 2002** £3.99
This is brilliant, overtaking its Sangiovese counterpart
(see above) this year for intensity with its blackcurranty
exuberance of fruit and refreshing bounce of flavour –
amazing at this price. **BEST BUY**

FRANCE

8 **Château Blanca, AC Bordeaux 2000** £4.49
Friendly ordinary claret has good 'typicity' – by which I
mean it tastes like claret – and at this price represents an
affordable chance of a reminder of the style of Bordeaux.

CHILE

8 **Cono Sur Pinot Noir 2001** £4.99
Ripe, raspberry perfume rises from this alluring, earthily
delicious Pinot, which makes a rare success of rendering
this difficult grape into a wine of concentration and
character. The 2002 is equally good.

ITALY

8 **Inycon Aglianico 2001** £4.99
This is one of the better wines in the Inycon range from
Sicily. It's a big meaty red with 13.5 per cent alcohol and
starts a bit raisiny, but in the glass it quickly blooms into
a fleshy, earthy and relishable food-matcher – pizza, for
once, comes to mind.

SOUTH AFRICA

9 Goats do Roam 2002   **£4.99**

Terrific, deliciously yielding, but robust, firm and ripe
bargain red is made largely from South Africa's
indigenous grape variety, the Pinotage. The odd name is a
tilt at French Côtes du Rhône but also celebrates the fact
that the maker, Charles Back, is a goat farmer as well. A
herd of 600 of them roam his Fairview estate, and some
of South Africa's best cheese is made from their milk.

RED WINES   OVER £5

AUSTRALIA

8 Wolf Blass Shiraz
   Cabernet Sauvignon 2001   **£6.99**

Lovely, silky, rich blend of blackcurrant and spice in this
masterly middleweight from the vineyard founded 35
years ago by German immigrant Wolfgang Blass. A well-
known brand, but not one that is resting on its laurels.

S AFRICA

8 Spice Route Pinotage 2000   **£8.99**

From the Fairview Estate of Goats do Roam fame (see
above), this is a gorgeous, cushion-of-fruit, fabulously
ripe and exhilarating red from the Cape's own indigenous
grape variety. Best Pinotage on the market.

SPAIN

7 Viña Cana Rioja Crianza 1999   **£5.99**

Muscular red with gripping fruit and a nice minty
background – soft and typically Spanish and somehow
summery, just right for glugging with barbecued fish or
an ambitious paella.

ROSÉ WINES   £3 TO £5

FRANCE

9 Côte Sauvage Dry Rosé 2002   £3.99
Note the 'dry'. This Vin de Pays d'Oc, proclaiming itself
made from the region's workhorse grape the Cinsault, is
indeed dry and also splendidly laden with raspberry-
strawberry fruit and a high level of refreshingness – and
a very jolly magenta colour. Very good buy.

DRY WHITE WINES   £3 TO £5

AUSTRALIA

7 Jindalee Chardonnay 2002   £4.99
Hint of well-buttered scrambled egg in this strong-
flavoured, 14-per-cent-alcohol heavyweight at a fair
price. 'Jindalee' rather boringly means 'bare hill' in
Aborigine.

8 Oxford Landing Chardonnay 2002   £4.99
Dependable, popular brand, which is always an
interesting and rather exotic glassful, with pineappley
fruit and the power to refresh.

ITALY

8 Chiaro di Luna Bianco di Custoza 2002   £3.99
A Veronese wine very similar indeed to Soave – and good
Soave at that. Fresh, bright and summery lightweight that
would go down well with an aromatic risotto.

7 Pinot Grigio del Veneto 2002   £4.99
Perpetually trendy PG comes in its humblest guise from
the all-embracing Veneto region of north-east Italy but
this isn't at all a bad one, with enough fruit and
smokiness to make it interesting.

8   **Danie de Wet Chardonnay 2002**   **£4.49**

Can't resist this perfect name for a winemaker, and this everyday, fresh, bright and well-extracted Chardonnay is pretty irresistible too at the price.

S AFRICA

D\RY WHITE WINES	OVER £5

9   **Argento Chardonnay 2002**   **£5.03**

This is a well-known brand from Nicolas Catena that delivers more flavour and interest than just about any other Chardonnay I can think of at the price – lush, peachy stuff but with a pure, bright fruitiness that brings a smile. It's a safe bet and seems to be on sale just about everywhere.

ARGENTINA

9   **Somerfield White Burgundy 2002**   **£5.49**

Excellent, crisp but layered and complex Chardonnay from Nuits-St-Georges producer Georges Desiré. Good white burgundy at this sort of price is a rarity.

8   **Somerfield Chablis 2001**   **£6.99**

I have had several really awful bottles of Chablis in the last year, either dirty-tasting or over the hill, regardless of price. This one is a refreshing example, brightly crisp but well endowed with that distinctive 'leafy' Chablis perfume and flinty style. Made by the estimable La Chablisienne co-operative and worth the money.

FRANCE

9   **Montana Unoaked East Coast Chardonnay 2002**   **£5.99**

This is a glittering wine, lemon-gold in colour and with a matching citrussy background to the lively, pineapple fruit. It echoes the unique fresh-yet-intense style that so marks out New Zealand's great Sauvignon wines, and as such is another happy variation on this ever-extending theme.

NEW ZEALAND

SOUTH AFRICA

8 Porcupine Ridge Sauvignon Blanc 2002   £5.49
I would like to say this has prickly fruit or something but I had better stick to the point and report that this a deliciously lively and brisk, grassy-fresh Sauvignon of real quality and at a good price.

**8 Somerfield Western Cape Limited Release
Chardonnay 2001   £5.49**
A whopper of a wine, this, with a butteriness that is overt and yet has the restraint of Burgundy rather than the in-your-face Australian style. Plenty of ripe (14 per cent alcohol) pineapple and peach fruit to construct a proper special-occasion wine at a sensible price.

SPAIN

10 Torres Viña Esmeralda 2002   £5.49
This is one of Spain's great wines. It's grown in the broiling vineyards of Penedes in the hinterland of Barcelona and yet tastes a lot like the sort of aromatic wine that is made in the cool northern vineyards of Alsace. The magic formula is Muscat grapes, fermented out to make a grapey but dry wine plus a measure of Gewürztraminer for spice and exotic smokiness. Result, a marvellous tangy, aromatic refresher of great character and quality at a keen price. Screwcap bottle and modest 11 per cent alcohol.   **BEST BUY**

Tesco

Britain's biggest retailer is also the country's biggest wine merchant, shifting one out of every seven bottles of wine we buy for drinking at home. It is just as well, therefore, that Tesco's wine range is as good as it is.

A bit like New Labour, Tesco's wine department is always brimming with initiatives. Besides the usual mantras about value for money and 'consumer choice', Tesco has in the last year espoused causes including organic wines and, rather more radically, screwcap wines.

Cork taint in wines has become such a problem that Tesco has decided to take a position. 'We cannot sit back and ignore anything that reduces our customers' enjoyment of wine, or at worst puts novices off drinking wine,' says the chain's product development manager Lindsay Talas. So Tesco has now launched a wittily named 'Unwind' screwcap range of wines which, says Lindsay, are of 'unadulterated, untainted varietal character produced from the most popular grape varieties'.

The first dozen or so to go on the shelf are all priced at £4.99, and Tesco has made a big – and largely successful – effort to 'break down the misconception that screwcap equals cheap and nasty wine' by designing their own special bottles and labels for the purpose.

Tesco says these wines, which are among a total of many more screwcaps it now sells, are going down very well with customers – even among those 'who shunned the idea in the past.' It is selling millions every month, and is now persuading suppliers that it would be a good idea to go over to screwcaps. And when Britain's biggest retailer of everything (including wine) tells its suppliers something is a good idea, those suppliers tend to agree.

Because it is such a vast network of stores – 566 at the last count – ranging from relatively dinky Metro outlets to hypermarkets bigger than football pitches, the extent of the wine range carried does vary from branch to branch. This does mean you cannot count on finding all of the wines mentioned here in every branch. But you can if you wish check whether your local store carries any particular wine by ringing the freecall central Customer Service line on 0800 505555.

Tesco also happens to have one of the best-designed websites, at **www.tesco.com**. It features regularly changing offers of mixed cases, at prices reduced by as much as a third from what you would pay in store. Online shoppers should take note, but so should any wine enthusiast planning a visit to a store, because the special offers online are quite separate from those promoted in the supermarkets themselves.

RED WINES   £3 TO £5

ARGENTINA

8 Picajuan Peak Sangiovese 2002   £4.01
Fresh, cherry-fruit but warm-hearted, soft red from the grape of Chianti by great La Agricola estate in Mendoza is a perennial bargain.

6 Unwind Tempranillo   £4.99
A big, alcoholic red at 14 per cent, but it seems rather hard and overheated. Not the best in the Unwind screwcap range.

AUSTRALIA

**7 Tesco Australian Finest Reserve
Merlot 2002**   £4.99
Purply, sweet-centred, meaty red.

7 Tempus Two Shiraz 2002   £4.99
Blackcurrant style with cushiony, minty fruit – more subtle than the usual dollopy Shiraz.

7 Unwind Shiraz   £4.99
Big, burnt wine will appeal to macho drinkers. Screwcap bottle.

CHILE

4 Unwind Pinot Noir   £4.99
I am a fan of Tesco's Unwind screwcap range but not of this lean, woody and unlovable red.

S AFRICA

8 Tesco South African Pinotage 2002   £3.99
Pruny and characterful, squishy-fruit, young red from Cape's own grape is worth a try.

USA

7 Tesco Californian Red Zinfandel £3.99
A crowd-pleaser of a wine, this is soft but not sweet, ripe
but not cooked – clever stuff at the price.

RED WINES   OVER £5

8 Mount Hurtle Cabernet Sauvignon 2000 £5.99
Made by legendary Geoff Merrill, a brightly clean-
tasting, lush, blackcurranty item that seems very easy to
drink – good wine-bar red for drinking on its own as well
as with food.

9 Hardy's Varietal Range Reserve
Cabernet Sauvignon 2001 £6.49
Rather an elegant Cabernet with restrained but
deliciously pure cassis, cushiony fruit. Dare one say it is
almost in the Bordeaux style?

8 Hardy's Varietal Range Reserve
Shiraz 2001 £6.49
Screwcap bottle but a serious wine with pitch-dark
colour and big whack of ripe fruit (14 per cent alcohol)
with a dark chocolate heart. Winter warmer.

8 Lindemans Reserve Shiraz 2001 £6.99
This is one up from the ubiquitous Lindemans Bin 35
Shiraz, and is a lot more interesting for the extra quid,
with hefty liquorice and lots of nuance and grip.

8 Tyrrells Old Winery Pinot Noir 2002 £6.99
Australia usually struggles to make decent Pinot but this
hits the spot – proper strawberry-cherry smell and that
authentic silkiness.

AUSTRALIA

8 **Thorn-Clarke Barossa Valley**
Nebbiolo 2002 £6.99
Nebbiolo is the grape that makes Italy's Barolo, and this
version has something of the spiky-spirity nature of the
original. A good gimmicky wine, and much cheaper than
proper Barolo.

8 **Penfolds Thomas Hyland**
Cabernet Sauvignon 2001 £8.99
Deep purple young-looking colour but a nicely rounded-
out wine with suggestions of blackcurrant tart and lots of
cream – rich and balanced and worth the premium price.

7 **La Palmeria Merlot Gran Reserva 2001** £9.99
Top-of-the-heap Chilean is dense in colour and massive
with ripe fruit (14 per cent alcohol), and showing signs of
turning into a lovely glassful, but you should keep it at
least until 2006 to deliver what it's really capable of.

8 **Beaujolais Villages Combes aux**
Jacques Louis Jadot 2001 £5.87
If you're curious to know what good Beaujolais is really
like, try this deliciously bouncy, juicy and refreshing red
from one of Burgundy's great trading companies, Louis
Jadot, which has made a great wine in 2001 – much
better than its effort in 2000.

7 **Tesco Finest South African**
Shiraz-Cabernet 2002 £5.49
Decent, gripping, middleweight, minty red with plenty of
grunt (14 per cent alcohol).

AUSTRALIA

CHILE

FRANCE

S AFRICA

Tesco

S AFRICA

🍷7 Beyerskloof Synergy Cape Blend 2001 £8.99
Spirity nose on this solid, concentrated mélange of
Pinotage with Merlot and Cabernet Sauvignon has a
relishable silkiness now, and the maker reckons it will
improve for the next decade.

USA

🍷7 Pepi Merlot 2000 £6.99
Ignore the pretentious 1950s retro label and enjoy the
good, honest, black-cherry fruit.

**🍷8 Fetzer Vineyards Barrel Select
Pinot Noir 2001** £9.99
California is good at Pinot Noir, and Fetzer, a sort of
semi-organic set-up, does everything well, so this is a
dependable buy, though not cheap.

ROSÉ WINES	£3 TO £5

AUSTRALIA

🍷7 Tesco Unwind Rosé 2002 £4.99
Plenty of bright magenta colour, a good measure of
alcohol at 13 per cent, and an interesting whiff of toffee
on the nose. This is no fleeting flyweight but a hefty,
lingering summer-fruit wine with unusual dimension – all
in a screwcap bottle.

USA

🍷6 Tesco Californian Blush Zinfandel 2002 £3.99
Curious confection has a fleshy colour, flowery pong and
rosy fruitiness – will appeal to drinkers who like
Smarties.

You can study the list at home before braving the supermarket itself – or just order the wines for home delivery anyway. You pay £4.95 for delivery, but it's free if your order is worth £75 or more.

Of course for the large percentage of us who don't live within reasonable distance of a Waitrose – there are none in Scotland or north of Newark in England and only one in Wales (Monmouth) – mail order is the only answer anyway. Ring (Freephone) 0800 188881 or look online at **www.waitrose.com/wines**.

RED WINES   UNDER £3

FRANCE

9 **Cuvée Chasseur Vin de Pays de
L'Hérault 2002**   £2.99
Crunchy, fresh, young red from the warm South seems
amazingly good at this rock-bottom price.

ITALY

9 **Tria Syrah Sicilia 2002**   £2.99
Opaque, near-black wine has a matching black, tarry
heart to its flavour but lots of cheery Syrah fruit besides
– amazing value.

8 **Trinacria Sicilia Rosso 2002**   £2.99
Typical warmly spicy and approachable Sicilian red, and
typically good value for money.

RED WINES   £3 TO £5

ARGENTINA

8 **La Boca Malbec-Bonarda 2002**   £3.99
Easy-drinking, Italian-style, vigorously ripe glugger at an
easy price. Although the Malbec grape is an Argentine
speciality, I do think it does better when blended with a
'softening' variety like Bonarda – especially in the more
basic wines.

AUSTRALIA

7 **First Step Merlot 2002**   £4.99
This seems rather austere for a basic Aussie wine, with
residual tannin, but there is pleasing black-cherry fruit
behind the grip – and 14 per cent alcohol.

7 **Jindalee Shiraz 2002**   £4.99
The interest here is in the nice crisp 'entry' to the flavour
– a standard, big, soft Shiraz with an edge to the fruit that
impresses.

8 **Château Haut d'Allard 2001** £5.69
From the Côtes de Bourg in Bordeaux, a Merlot-dominated, darkly ripe and rounded, blackberry claret already drinking well.

8 **Beaujolais Villages Combes aux Jacques Louis Jadot 2001** £5.99
If you're curious to know what good Beaujolais is really like, try this deliciously bouncy, juicy and refreshing red from one of Burgundy's great trading companies, Louis Jadot, which has made a great wine in 2001 – much better than its effort in 2000.

7 **Côtes du Rhône, Max Chapoutier 2001** £5.99
Surprisingly light wine from this famed organic producer, but there's no shortage of warm, spicy flavour.

8 **Ermitage du Pic Saint-Loup 2001** £5.99
A perennial wine at Waitrose for many years, this splendid Languedoc red is mainly Syrah and has a well-contrived mix of soft spice and firm grip – and a hefty 14.5 per cent alcohol.

8 **Château Cazal-Viel Cuvée des Fées 2000** £6.99
From the Languedoc AC of St Chinian, a Syrah wine that contrives to taste a lot like expensive Rhône counterparts such as Cornas – dark, spicy, red wine with silkiness and grip that will no doubt age gracefully.

7 **Saumur-Champigny Château de Targé 2000** £6.99
Assertively flavoured Loire red has notably bright, pure flavours. Scores for distinctiveness, though not cheap.

FRANCE

8 Château Segonzac 2001 £7.99

This is a well-known estate of the Bordeaux AC Premières Côtes de Blaye and has made a well-structured, complete wine in this goodish vintage – very decent claret.

9 Corbières Domaine de Courtilles 2000 £7.99

Hugely concentrated, lush, red-berry fruit in this oaked reserve wine from a popular Midi AC – terrific wine with 14 per cent alcohol.

**8 Côtes de Beaune Villages,
Louis Jadot 1999** £9.99

Silky style to this mature Burgundy which has ideal marriage of earthiness and sweet, summer-soft fruit.

GREECE

8 Tsantali Cabernet Sauvignon 2000 £5.99

Deep purple, nice ripe and balanced red from Greece's best-known quality winemaker.

PORTUGAL

8 Dourosa, Quinta de la Rosa 2001 £5.99

Made by a port estate in the Douro Valley that specialises in making table wine, this is from the same grapes that go into the fortified wine and has recognisable porty flavours – without the headache factor.

8 Trincadeira, JP Ramos 2001 £6.99

Oaked, intense, black-fruit wine with typical Portuguese (Alentejo region) minty, eucalyptus-glycerine style – distinctive and delicious with meats and baked fish.

10 Excelsior Estate Paddock Shiraz 2002   £5.99
Near-perfect rendering of cushiony-fruit, soft, but tinglingly gripping, bright red-fruit Shiraz. It has an intriguing white-chocolate whiff, tremendous ripeness and background spice and an impressive completeness. Clearly made by a genius.   **BEST BUY**

**9 Thabani Cabernet Sauvignon/
Merlot 2001   £5.99**
Conventional Bordeaux-type blend from Stellenbosch turns out to be an outstanding wine – lovely plump, darkly dense heavyweight, nevertheless with a light touch and well balanced between rich, creamy, cassis fruit and brisk acidity, with a potent 14.5 per cent alcohol.

8 Bellingham Cabernet Sauvignon 2001   £6.99
A straightforward midweight textbook Cabernet with a poise and easy charm that serve as a useful reminder that the Cape can often do this sort of wine so much better than Australia for the same kind of money.

7 Mas Collet Celler de Capçanes 2000   £5.99
Spirity nose on a big, spicy-fiery red of character with 14 per cent alcohol and satisfying aftertaste – for the macho drinker, good with suitably heated Mexican food.

8 Rivola Abadia Retuerta 2000   £7.99
Sweet vanilla nose on this luxury Rioja-style oaked red with the additional ingredient of smooth cassis in the flavour. Seriously good wine from the Ribera del Duero region for the same price as a modest reserva Rioja and definitely one to try.

SOUTH AFRICA

SPAIN

ROSÉ WINES   £3 TO £5

AUSTRALIA

7 **Banrock Station White Shiraz 2002**   £4.99
It's not white, it's about the colour of smoked salmon,
and it has a likeable balance of the usual strawberry fruit
and fresh crispness. Not bad – and every bottle sold
generates a donation towards the conservation of
Australia's endangered wetlands.

FRANCE

8 **Waitrose Rosé d'Anjou 2002**   £3.79
Cheery, brightly coloured Loire pink has rose-petal pong
and easy summery fruit. You could call it 'medium dry'
(Waitrose do) but it isn't unrefreshing. Why pay more for
rosé?

DRY WHITE WINES   UNDER £3

AUSTRALIA

10 **Broken Bridge**
Chardonnay-Colombard 2002   £2.99
I am at a loss to know how Waitrose can sell wine this
good at under £3. Okay, it's bottled in the UK (comes
over in a bulk tank) but it has a splendid apple-blossom
scent, middling weight of fresh appley-peachy fruit and a
satisfying finish. Can't fault it.   **BEST BUY**

DRY WHITE WINES	£3 TO £5

ARGENTINA

7 **La Boca Torrontes-Chardonnay 2002** £3.99
Interesting blend of grapey-spicy Torrontes with crisp
Chardonnay makes for an enjoyable mild-mannered
aperitif wine.

8 **Etchart Privado Torrontes,**
High Andes Cafayate 2002 £4.99
Argentines are very proud of their high-altitude Andean
vineyards and all sorts of claims are made for the health-
giving properties of wines made there. This is certainly a
healthy wine, with spice and muscat grapiness but dry
and fresh.

AUSTRALIA

7 **Bear Crossing Sauvignon**
Blanc-Chardonnay 2002 £4.99
Clean and breezy, fresh, economy wine from a mix of
grapes I don't usually find very successful.

9 **First Step Chardonnay 2002** £4.99
Exotic tropical-fruit style to this rich and ripe (14 per
cent alcohol) budget wine. On re-tasting I liked it even
better.

CHILE

8 **San Andrés Chardonnay 2002** £3.99
Lots of colour and fleshy fruit here for the money – 'Nice
agricultural Chardonnay', it says in my note.

8 **Casillero del Diablo Chardonnay 2002** £4.99
Good vegetal wine with emphatic focused Chardonnay
flavours – true to the variety.

8 **Domaine de Planterieu 2002** £3.99
A Vin de Pays de Gascogne with lemon-gold colour, floral nose and zingy fruit. Excellent all round, and a modest 11.5 per cent alcohol.

8 **Waitrose Touraine Sauvignon Blanc 2002** £3.99
Great nose on this – gooseberry and grass with a hint of toffee – and a vibrant nettley rush of clean fruit with a tingle of spritz. Good value.

7 **Saint-Pourçain Réserve Spéciale 2002** £4.49
Tangy but not oversharp Loire bone-dry white has lots of interest.

8 **La Baume Viognier,**
Vin de Pays d'Oc 2002 £4.99
Big-brand southern Viognier has come up trumps this year with a proper unctuous-but-dry, exotically fruity and weighty standalone wine of 13.5 per cent alcohol.

8 **Mâcon-Villages Chardonnay,**
Cave de Prissé 2002 £4.99
Much better than expected, brightly clean, citrussy Chardonnay from the usually overpriced and under-fruited Mâcon appellations of southern Burgundy.

10 **Muscadet Côtes de Grandlieu sur Lie,**
Fief Guérin 2002 £4.99
There seems to be more good Muscadet around this year than I can ever remember before. The briny whiff fairly jumps out of the glass from this one, but it doesn't suffer from over-acidity – having lots of crisp but dimensional bright fruit and a lingering finish that leaves you pondering the flavours rather than wincing from too much citrus. **BEST BUY**

FRANCE

🍷8 **Muscat Sec, Vin de Pays des Côtes Catalanes 2002** £4.99

A real sweet and spicy, grapey nose on this, but the fruit is dry, aromatic and contemplative.

GERMANY

🍷8 **Almond Grove Dry Riesling 2001** £3.99

Dry indeed, but great value for all that racy brisk fruit. This is one of the many German wines now sold under New-World type names, presumably in an attempt to overcome market resistance to anything Teutonic.

HUNGARY

🍷7 **Riverview Sauvignon Blanc 2002** £3.99

Brisk, nettly wine contrives to have gentle acidity – an easy-finishing dry white for those who don't like their white wine too 'sharp'.

ITALY

🍷7 **Soave Classico Vigneto Colombara, Zenato 2002** £4.99

Good perfume – peach, lemon, blanched almonds – from this satisfying plump and ripe, big-name Soave that's above average for the price.

PORTUGAL

🍷8 **Vinho Verde Quinta de Simaens 2001** £4.99

The characterful 'green wine' of Portugal's Minho Valley has rather gone out of fashion of late but this natural (unsweetened), faintly spritzy, lemony item might help revive the vogue.

S AFRICA

🍷8 **Danie de Wet Chardonnay 2002** £4.49

Can't resist this perfect name for a winemaker, and this everyday fresh, bright and well-extracted Chardonnay is pretty irresistible too at the price.

Waitrose

SPAIN

8 **Rueda Palacio de Bornos Verdejo 2002** £4.99
There's a true whiff of nectar off this fascinating dry white from the excellent Rueda region. The fruit has a combination of the nettliness of the Sauvignon grape and the peach of Chardonnay – but it all comes from the Verdejo grapes, indigenous to Rueda.

DRY WHITE WINES	OVER £5

ARGENTINA

8 **Tarrazas Chardonnay 2002** £5.99
Good, straight Chardonnay, with crisp, direct, pure fruit and mineral freshness.

10 **Catena Agrelo Vineyards Chardonnay 2001** £9.99
Nicholas Catena has achieved iconic status for the Chardonnay that bears his name. It is amazingly consistent year after year, and the price has escalated only modestly. This is a chance to taste the veritable apogee of Argentine Chardonnay – rich, pure, mineral wine of memorable character. **BEST BUY**

AUSTRALIA

8 **Basedow Barossa Valley Semillon 2001** £5.99
Intense gold colour and that distinctive banana-pineapple whiff of Semillon, then a positive hamper of fruit sensations in the mouth – mysterious, delicious, tropical-style dry white.

8 **Yalumba Y Viognier 2002** £6.99
Surprisingly restrained, unoaked Viognier with welcome freshness and nicely targeted fruit. Very easy to drink – but note the 14 per cent alcohol. Terrific perfume.

CHILE

7 **Gracia Chardonnay Reserve Ausente 2001** **£5.99**
Exaggerated toffee nose and corresponding butterscotch
depths to the fruit – a very rich wine to suit a particular
kind of taste.

8 **Château Thieuley 2002** **£6.69**
Enticing fruit-blossom scent from this elegant, dry white
Bordeaux and a satisfyingly complex basket of flavours
to match.

8 **Petit Chablis, La Chablisienne 2002** **£6.99**
Promising flinty nose on this Chardonnay from the
elusive Petit Chablis appellation but quite a rich style to
the fruit, though with the distinctive stony Chablis
highlights – very nice easy-drinker in a screwcap bottle at
an unusually reasonable price.

FRANCE

9 **Saint-Véran Les Plantés,
Cave de Prissé 2002** **£6.99**
Pale-gold colour, nice melon and ripe apple Chardonnay
aroma and a whack of ripe (13 per cent alcohol), lush,
apple-pie fruit from this mineral Mâconnais wine – a
great surprise to me, as I have long harboured suspicions
about the appellation.

10 **Château Carsin Cuvée Prestige 2001** **£7.99**
Dry white Bordeaux is not as fashionable as it used to be,
but this just has to be tried. The nose, evoking bananas
with cream and fresh pineapple among other things, is
divine, and the fruit is lush, exotic, suggestive of new oak
and utterly enchanting. A seducer's wine!   **BEST BUY**

Waitrose

**9 Alsace Gewürztraminer Classique,
Josmeyer 2001** £9.99

Beautiful, spicy-lychee, rich, plump, smoky classic Gewürz from an individual grower whose wines just don't appear in supermarkets.

8 Chablis Domaine William Fèvre 2001 £9.99

Smart wine in which you can easily imagine you can detect the legendary 'green shot with gold' of Chablis – a metaphor that is believed to apply equally to colour and flavour. This oak-aged wine is in the rich style with a creamy Chardonnay nose but still has the thrill of gunflint in the fruit. Lovely stuff.

**9 Domaine de la Baume Blanc
Viognier-Chardonnay 2000** £9.99

Blending Viognier and Chardonnay always seems fruitless to me, but this one makes me think otherwise. The effect in this Languedoc experiment is a gold colour, extravagant vanilla-spearmint-tropical fruit nose, and a balanced but voluptuous peachy, ripe, dry wine of real character. Gorgeous, 14.5 per cent alcohol, and worth the money.

FRANCE

8 Rupperstberger Nussbien Riesling 2001 £5.79

Extraordinary nose of pineapple on this unexpectedly lush QbA Rheinpfalz wine – delicious light aperitif style.

**9 Ockfener Bockstein Riesling,
Dr Wagner 2001** £5.99

Pure, heavenly Moselle with apple-pie richness amidst the raciness of the Riesling fruit – really a bargain at this price.

GERMANY

GERMANY

9 Bassermann Jordan Riesling 2001 £6.49

Lots of colour and a particular plump, ripe style of Rheinpfalz Riesling that fairly sings.

8 Serriger Herrenberg Riesling Kabinett, Bert Simon 1998 £6.99

Lush, appley, crisp-finishing Moselle of memorable purity.

NEW ZEALAND

9 Villa Maria Private Bin Pinot Gris 2002 £6.99

Lively Kiwi variation on Italy's inexplicably trendy Pinot Grigio is miles better than anything I've had from Italy itself. Lovely, smoky, aromatic but fresh dry white of character, with an awesome (but not noticeable) 14.5 per cent alcohol and a screwcap.

8 One Tree Unoaked Chardonnay 2002 £7.99

It's unoaked but by no means spartan and I detected a lush toffee-apple note in the midst of the lavish ripe (14 per cent alcohol) fruit – great wine in a screwcap bottle.

SOUTH AFRICA

10 Jordan Chardonnay 2002 £7.99

I shouldn't say eight quid is cheap for a bottle of wine but in this case I must. This is the ideal balance of butterscotch richness and apple-mineral Chardonnay fruit – a luxury dry white with feel-good factor. Nothing from Australia, or anywhere else, comes near it at this price. **BEST BUY**

8 Steenberg Semillon 2002 £7.99

From the grand Steenberg vineyard at Constantia in the suburbs of Cape Town, an extravagant oaked, tropical-fruit dry white of great class – and 15 per cent alcohol.

S AFRICA

♍8 Kumala Journey's End Chardonnay 2002 £14.99
Kumala is the leading brand from South Africa but I am
not greatly enamoured of their range – except for this
pricey flagship bottle, which is pure gold in colour and
flavour, an opulent pure Burgundy-style of arresting
quality.

SPAIN

♍10 Torres Viña Esmeralda 2002 £5.49
This is one of Spain's great wines. It's grown in the
broiling vineyards of Penedes in the hinterland of
Barcelona and yet tastes a lot like the sort of aromatic
wine that is made in the cool northern vineyards of
Alsace. The magic formula is Muscat grapes, fermented
out to make a grapey but dry wine plus a measure of
Gewürztraminer for spice and exotic smokiness. Result,
a marvellous tangy, aromatic refresher of great character
and quality at a keen price. Screwcap bottle and modest
11 per cent alcohol. **BEST BUY**

USA

♍8 Wente Chardonnay 2001 £7.49
Creamy Californian with lush seductive fruit – you warm
to it.

SWEET WHITE WINES · OVER £5

9 **Château Les Sablines, Monbazillac 1998** £6.99
Rich in colour, texture and flavour, a very good value pud
wine from the same grapes that go into hugely expensive
Sauternes, a few miles west of Monbazillac.

8 **Domaine des Forges,**
Coteaux du Layon Chaume 2001 £9.99
Gold colour and evident botrytis ('noble rot') on this
classic Loire stickie from Chenin Blanc grapes picked
very late in the year in the Loire Valley.

9 **Hallgartner Jungfer Riesling Auslese,**
Hans Lang 1999 £9.99
Ripe apples and honey notes on the nose of this lush
Rheingau late-picked beauty. Wine like this keeps and
develops for many years but this one is already divinely
ready to sip with, say, foie gras or blue cheese, or just on
its own. Note only 8.5 per cent alcohol.

FORTIFIED WINES · £3 TO £5

8 **Waitrose Fino sherry** £4.99
Long-aged, dry, pale sherry is fresh and good value. Not
a wine with a lot of acidity, so should appeal to more
conservative tastes and has 16.5 per cent alcohol.

FORTIFIED WINES · OVER £5

8 **Henriques & Henriques**
Monte Seco Madeira (50 cl) £6.49
Gold-coloured wine with a dreamy heathery perfume and
lovely rancio flavours. It is a dry, fresh kind of wine for
drinking chilled and has 19 per cent alcohol.

9 **Waitrose Solera Jerezana**
Manzanilla sherry £5.99

Eclipsing most other Manzanilla at this price, this is the perfect embodiment of the bone-dry, briny-perfumed, tangy, palate-twanging pale sherry of Sanlucar. Fabulously stimulating and refreshing sherry with 17 per cent alcohol to drink chilled from a decent-sized glass.

10 **Waitrose Solera Jerezana Dry**
Amontillado sherry £5.99

Note that word 'dry'. Most supermarket Amontillados are horribly sweetened and vile, but this really is an absolute beauty – aromatic, nutty, crammed with the untrammelled flavours of natural dry sherry – a wonderful wine at this price, with 20 per cent alcohol.

BEST BUY

10 **Waitrose Solera Jerezana Dry Oloroso**
sherry £5.99

Deep, amber colour to this rare sherry. *Oloroso* means 'fragrant' in Spanish and does not, contrary to popular belief, mean 'sweet'. This is indeed a dry wine, but it's by no means arid. It's piled high with balanced raisiny, nutty flavours with 20 per cent alcohol and perfect weight – a flagship for true dark sherry. Please try it – at this price it's a very inexpensive route to discovering a whole new wine-drinking experience. **BEST BUY**

9 **Waitrose Solera Jerezano**
Rich Cream sherry £5.99

Lovely, burnt-amber colour and a perfectly 'dry', nutty-dried-fruit aroma. 'Rich Cream' doesn't mean sweet, it means velvetised, with an undercurrent of fruit-cake enrichment. Absolutely gorgeous sherry to drink cool as an aperitif or at room temperature with after-dinner cheese or cake.

Glossary

Wine labels convey a lot of information, some of it helpful. Under a combination of UK and EU regulations, the quantity and alcoholic strength of the contents must be displayed, as must the country of origin. And besides the wines from the traditional regions and appellations of France (Bordeaux, Burgundy etc.), Italy (Barolo, Chianti) and Spain (Rioja, Navarra), the label is also very likely to bear the name of the grape or grapes involved. In the mass market, grape names such as Chardonnay and Shiraz now count for a lot more than this or that vineyard, region or even nation.

So, this glossary includes the names of more than 60 different grape varieties along with brief descriptions of their characteristics. The varietal name on a label tells you more than anything else about what to expect of the wine.

Other items in this vocabulary include short summaries of the regions and appellations of recommended wines and some of the many label designations given to the style, alleged quality and regulatory classifications.

Finally, I have tried to explain in simple and rational terms the many peculiar words I use in trying to convey the characteristics of wines described. 'Delicious' might need no further qualification, but the likes of 'bouncy', 'green' and 'liquorous' probably do.

A

abboccato – Medium-dry white wine style. Italy, especially Orvieto.

AC – *See* Appellation d'Origine Contrôlée.

acidity – To be any good, every wine must have the right level of acidity. It gives wine the element of dryness or sharpness it needs to prevent cloying sweetness or dull wateriness. If there is too much acidity, wine tastes raw or acetic (vinegary). Winemakers strive to create balanced acidity – either by cleverly controlling the natural processes, or by adding sugar and acid to correct imbalances.

aftertaste – The flavour that lingers in the mouth after swallowing the wine.

Aglianico – Black grape variety of southern Italy. It has romantic associations. When the ancient Greeks first colonised Italy in the seventh century BC, it was with the prime purpose of planting it as a vineyard (the Greek name for Italy was *Oenotria* – land of cultivated vines). The name for the vines the Greeks brought with them was *Ellenico* (as in *Hellas,* Greece), from which Aglianico is the modern rendering. To return to the point, these ancient vines, especially in the arid volcanic landscapes of Basilicata, produce excellent dark, earthy and highly distinctive wines. A name to look out for.

Agriculture biologique – On French wine labels, an indication that the wine has been made by organic methods.

Albariño – White grape variety of Spain that makes intriguingly perfumed fresh and spicy dry wines, especially in esteemed Rias Baixas region.

Almansa – DO winemaking region of Spain inland from Alicante, making great-value red wines.

alcohol – The alcohol levels in wines are expressed in terms of alcohol by volume ('abv'), that is, the percentage of the volume of the wine that is common, or ethyl, alcohol. A typical wine at 12 per cent abv is thus 12 parts alcohol and, in effect, 88 parts fruit juice.

The question of how much alcohol we can drink without harming ourselves in the short or long term is an impossible one to answer, but there is more or less general agreement among scientists that small amounts of alcohol are good for us, even if the only evidence of this is actuarial – the fact that mortality statistics show teetotallers live significantly shorter lives than moderate drinkers. According to the Department of Health, there are 'safe limits' to the amount of alcohol we should drink weekly. These limits are measured in units of alcohol, with a small glass of wine taken to be one unit. Men are advised that 28 units a week is the most they can drink without risk to health, and for women (whose liver function differs from men because of metabolic differences) the figure is 21 units.

If you wish to measure your consumption closely, note that a standard 75 cl bottle of wine at 12 per cent alcohol contains nine units. A bottle of German Moselle at 8 per cent alcohol has only six units, but a bottle of Australian Chardonnay at 14 per cent has 10.5.

Alentejo – Wine region of southern Portugal (immediately north of the Algarve), with a fast-improving reputation, especially for sappy, keen reds from local grape varieties including Aragones, Castelão and Trincadeira grapes.

Alsace – France's easternmost wine-producing region lies between the Vosges Mountains and the River Rhine, with Germany beyond. These conditions make for the production of some of the world's most delicious and fascinating white wines, always sold under the name of their constituent grapes. Pinot Blanc is the most affordable – and is well worth looking out for. The 'noble' grape varieties of the region are Gewürztraminer, Muscat, Riesling and Tokay Pinot Gris and they are always made on a single-variety basis. The richest, most exotic wines are those from individual grand cru vineyards, which are named on the label. Some *vendange* *tardive* (late harvest) wines are made, but tend to be expensive. All the wines are sold in tall, slim green bottles known as *flûtes* that closely resemble those of the Mosel, and the names of producers and grape varieties are often German too, so it is widely assumed that Alsace wines are German in style, if not in nationality. But this is not the case in either particular. Alsace wines are dry and quite unique in character – and definitely French.

amontillado – *See* Sherry.

aperitif – If a wine is thus described, I believe it will give more pleasure before a meal than with one. Crisp, low-alcohol German wines and other delicately flavoured whites (including many dry Italians) are examples.

Appellation d'Origine Contrôlée – Commonly abbreviated to AC or AOC, this is the system under which quality wines are defined in France. About a third of the country's vast annual output qualifies, and there are more than 400 distinct AC zones. The declaration of an AC on the label signifies that the wine meets standards concerning location of vineyards and wineries, grape varieties and limits on harvest per hectare, methods of cultivation and vinification, and alcohol content. Wines are inspected and tasted by state-appointed committees. The one major aspect of any given wine that an AC cannot guarantee is that you will like it – but it certainly improves the chances.

Apulia – Anglicised name for Puglia.

Ardèche – Region of southern France to the west of the Rhône valley, home to a good vin de pays zone known as the Coteaux de L'Ardèche. Lots of decent-value reds from Syrah grapes, and some, less-interesting, dry whites.

Assyrtiko – White grape variety of Greece now commonly named on dry white wines, sometimes of great quality, from the mainland and islands.

Asti – Town and major winemaking centre in Piedmont, Italy.

The sparkling *(spumante)* sweet wines made from Moscato grapes are inexpensive and often delicious. Typical alcohol level is a modest 5 to 7 per cent.

attack – In wine tasting, the first impression made by the wine in the mouth.

auslese – German wine-quality designation. *See* QmP.

B

backbone – A personal item of wine-tasting terminology. It's the impression given by a well-made wine in which the flavours are a pleasure to savour at all three stages: initial sensation in the mouth; while being held in the mouth; in the aftertaste when the wine has been swallowed or spat out. Such a wine is held together by backbone.

Baga – Black grape variety indigenous to Portugal. Makes famously concentrated, juicy reds that get their deep colour from the grape's particularly thick skins. Look out for this name, now quite frequently quoted as the varietal on Portuguese wine labels. Often very good value for money.

balance – A big word in the vocabulary of wine tasting. Respectable wine must get two key things right: lots of fruitiness from the sweet grape juice, and plenty of acidity so the sweetness is 'balanced' with the crispness familiar in good dry whites and the dryness that marks out good reds. Some wines are noticeably 'well balanced' in that they have memorable fruitiness and the clean, satisfying 'finish' (last flavour in the mouth) that ideal acidity imparts.

Barbera – Black grape variety originally of Piedmont in Italy. Most commonly seen as Barbera d'Asti, the vigorously fruity red wine made around Asti – which is better known for sweet sparkling Asti Spumante. Barbera grapes are now being grown in South America, often producing a sleeker, smoother style than at home in Italy.

Bardolino – Once-fashionable, light red wine DOC of Veneto, north-west Italy. Bardolino is made principally from Corvina

Veronese grapes plus Rondinella, Molinara and Negrara. Best wines are supposed to be those labelled *classico,* and *superiore* is applied to those aged a year and having at least 11.5 per cent alcohol.

Barossa Valley – Famed vineyard region north of Adelaide, Australia, produces hearty reds principally from Shiraz, Cabernet Sauvignon and Grenache grapes, plus plenty of lush white wine from Chardonnay. Also known for limey, long-lived, mineral dry whites from Riesling grapes.

barrique – Barrel in French. *En barrique* on a wine label signifies the wine has been matured in oak.

Beaujolais – Unique red wines from the southern reaches of Burgundy, France, are made from Gamay grapes. Beaujolais nouveau, the new wine of each harvest, is released on the third Thursday of every November to much ballyhoo. It provides a friendly introduction to this deliciously bouncy, fleshily fruity wine style. Decent Beaujolais for enjoying during the rest of the year has lately become rather more expensive. If splashing out, go for Beaujolais Villages, from the region's better, northern vineyards. There are ten AC zones within the northern part of the region making wines under their own names. Known as the *crus,* these are Brouilly, Chénas, Chiroubles, Côte de Brouilly, Fleurie, Juliénas, Morgon, Moulin à Vent, Regnié and St Amour and produce most of the very best wines of the region – at prices a pound or two higher than for Beaujolais Villages.

Beaumes de Venise – Village near Châteauneuf du Pape in France's Rhône valley, famous for sweet and alcoholic wine from Muscat grapes. Delicious, grapey wines. A small number of growers also make strong (sometimes rather tough) red wines under the village name.

Beaune – One of the two winemaking centres (the other is Nuits St Georges) at the heart of Burgundy in France. Three of the region's humbler appellations take the name of the town: Côtes de Beaune, Côtes de Beaune Villages and Hautes

Côtes de Beaune. Wines made under these ACs are often, but by no means always, good value for money.

berry fruit – Some red wines deliver a burst of flavour in the mouth that corresponds to biting into a newly picked berry – strawberry, blackberry, etc. So a wine described as having berry fruit (by this writer, anyway) has freshness, liveliness, immediate appeal.

bianco – White wine, Italy.

Bical – White grape variety principally of Dão region of northern Portugal. Not usually identified on labels, because most of it goes into inexpensive sparkling wines. Can make still wines of very refreshing crispness.

biodynamics – A cultivation method taking the organic approach several steps further. Biodynamic winemakers plant and tend their vineyards according to a date and time calendar 'in harmony' with the movements of the planets. Some of France's best-known wine estates subscribe, and many more are going that way. It might all sound bonkers, but it's salutary to learn that biodynamics is based on principles first described by a very eminent man, the Austrian educationist Rudolph Steiner. He's lately been in the news for having written, in 1919, that farmers crazy enough to feed animal products to cattle would drive the livestock 'mad'.

bite – In wine tasting, the impression on the palate of a wine with plenty of acidity and, often, tannin.

blanc – White wine, France.

blanc de blancs – White wine from white grapes, France. May seem to be stating the obvious, but some white wines (e.g. champagne) are made, partially or entirely, from black grapes.

blanc de noirs – White wine from black grapes, France. Usually sparkling (especially champagne) made from black Pinot Meunier and Pinot Noir grapes, with no Chardonnay or other white varieties.

blanco – White wine, Spain and Portugal.

Blauer Zweigelt – Black grape variety of Austria, making a large proportion of the country's red wines, some of excellent quality.

bodega – In Spain, a wine producer or wine shop.

Bonarda – Black grape variety of northern Italy. Now more widely planted in Argentina, where it makes rather elegant red wines, often representing great value.

botrytis – Full name, *botrytis cinerea,* is that of a beneficent fungus that can attack ripe grape bunches late in the season, shrivelling the berries to a gruesome-looking mess, which yields concentrated juice of prized sweetness. Cheerfully known as 'noble rot', this fungus is actively encouraged by winemakers in regions as diverse as Sauternes (in Bordeaux), Monbazillac (in Bergerac), the Rhine and Mosel valleys and South Australia to make ambrosial dessert wines.

bouncy – The feel in the mouth of a red wine with young, juicy fruitiness. Good Beaujolais is bouncy as are many north-west-Italian wines from Barbera and Dolcetto grapes.

Bourgogne Grand Ordinaire – Appellation of France's Burgundy region for 'ordinary' red wines from either Gamay or Pinot Noir grapes, or both. Some good-value wines, especially from the Buxy Co-operative in the southern Chalonnais area.

Bourgueil – Appellation of Loire Valley, France. Long-lived red wines from Cabernet Franc grapes.

briary – In wine-tasting, associated with the flavours of fruit from prickly bushes such as blackberries.

brûlé – Pleasant burnt-toffee taste or smell, as in crème brûlée.

brut – Driest style of sparkling wine. Originally French, for very dry champagnes specially developed for the British market, but now used for sparkling wines from all round the world.

Buzet – Little-seen AC of south-west France overshadowed by Bordeaux but producing some characterful ripe reds.

C

Cabardès – New AC (1998) for red and rosé wines from area north of Carcassonne, Aude, France. Principally Cabernet Sauvignon and Merlot grapes.

Cabernet franc – Black grape variety originally of France. It makes the light-bodied and keenly-edged red wines of the Loire Valley – such as Chinon and Saumur. And it is much grown in Bordeaux, especially in the appellation of St Emilion. Also now planted in Argentina, Australia and North America. Wines, especially in the Loire, are characterised by a leafy, sappy style and bold fruitiness. Most are best enjoyed young.

Cabernet Sauvignon – Black (or, rather, blue) grape variety now grown in virtually every wine-producing nation. When perfectly ripened, the grapes are smaller than many other varieties and have particularly thick skins. This means that when pressed Cabernet grapes have a high proportion of skin to juice – and that makes for wine with lots of colour and tannin. In Bordeaux, the grape's traditional home, the grandest Cabernet-based wines have always been known as *vins de garde* (wines to keep) because they take years, even decades, to evolve as the effect of all that skin extraction preserves the fruit all the way to magnificent maturity. But in today's impatient world, these grapes are exploited in modern winemaking techniques to produce the sublime flavours of mature Cabernet without having to hang around for lengthy periods awaiting maturation. While there's nothing like a fine, ten-year-old claret (and nothing quite as expensive), there are many excellent Cabernets from around the world that amply illustrate this grape's characteristics. Classic smells and flavours include blackcurrants, cedar wood, chocolate, tobacco – even violets.

Cahors – An AC of the Lot Valley in south-west France once famous for 'black wine'. This was a curious concoction of straightforward wine mixed with a soupy must, made by boiling up new-pressed juice to concentrate it (through evaporation) before fermentation. The myth is still perpetuated that Cahors wine continues to be made in this way, but production on this basis actually ceased 150 years ago. Cahors today is no stronger, or blacker, than the wines of neighbouring appellations.

Cairanne – Village of the appellation collectively known as the Côtes du Rhône Villages in south France. Cairanne is one of several villages entitled to put their name on the labels of wines made within their AC boundary, and the appearance of this name is quite reliably an indicator of a very good wine indeed.

Calatayud – DO (quality wine zone) near Zaragoza in the Aragon region of northern Spain where they're making some astonishingly good wines at bargain prices, mainly reds from Garnacha and Tempranillo grapes. These are the varieties that go into the light and oaky wines of Rioja, but in Calatayud, the wines are dark, dense and decidedly different.

cantina sociale – *See* Co-op.

Carignan – Black grape variety of Mediterranean France. It is rarely identified on labels, but is a major constituent of wines from the southern Rhône and Languedoc-Roussillon regions, especially the cheaper brands. Known as Carignano in Italy and Cariñena in Spain.

Carmenère – Black grape variety once widely grown in Bordeaux but abandoned due to cultivation problems. Lately revived in South America where it is producing fine wines.

cassis – As a tasting note, signifies a wine has a noticeable blackcurrant-concentrate flavour or smell. Much associated with the Cabernet Sauvignon grape.

Castelao – Portuguese black grape variety. Same as Periquita.

Catarratto – White grape variety of Sicily. In skilled hands it can make anything from keen, green-fruit dry whites to lush, oaked super-ripe styles. Also used for marsala.

cava – The sparkling wine of Spain. Most originates in Catalonia, but the Denominacion de Origen (DO) guarantee of authenticity is open to producers in many regions of the country. Much cava is very reasonably priced even though it is made by the same method as champagne – second fermentation in bottle, known in Spain as the metodo classico.

CdR – Côtes du Rhône.

Cépage – Grape variety, French. 'Cépage Merlot' on a label simply means the wine is made largely or exclusively from Merlot grapes.

Chablis – Northernmost AC of France's Burgundy region. Its dry white wines from Chardonnay grapes are known for their fresh and steely style, but the best wines also age very gracefully into complex classics.

Chambourcin – Sounds like a cream cheese but it's a relatively modern (1963) French hybrid black grape that makes some good non-appellation lightweight-but-concentrated reds in the Loire Valley and now some heftier versions in Australia.

Chardonnay – The world's most popular grape variety. Said to originate from the village of Chardonnay in the Mâconnais region of southern Burgundy, the vine is now planted in every wine-producing nation. Wines are commonly characterised by generous colour and sweet-apple smell, but styles range from lean and sharp to opulently rich. Australia started the craze for oaked Chardonnay, the gold-coloured, super-ripe, buttery 'upfront' wines that are a caricature of lavish and outrageously expensive Burgundies such as Meursault and Puligny-Montrachet. Rich to the point of egginess, these Aussie pretenders are now giving way to a sleeker, more minerally style with much less oak presence – if any at all. California and Chile, New Zealand and South Africa are competing hard to imitate the Burgundian style, and Australia's success in doing so.

Châteauneuf du Pape – Famed appellation centred on a picturesque village of the southern Rhône valley in France where in the 1320s French Pope Clement V had a splendid new château built for himself as a country retreat amidst his vineyards. The red wines of the AC, which can be made from 13 different grape varieties but principally Grenache, Syrah and Mourvèdre, are regarded as the best of the southern Rhône and have become rather expensive – but they can be sensationally good. Expensive white wines are also made.

Chenin blanc – White grape variety of the Loire Valley, France. Now also grown farther afield, especially in South Africa. Makes dry, soft white wines and also rich, sweet styles. Sadly, many low-cost Chenin wines are bland and uninteresting.

cherry – In wine-tasting, either a pale red colour or, more commonly, a smell or flavour akin to the sun-warmed, bursting sweet ripeness of cherries. Many Italian wines, from lightweights such as Bardolino and Valpolicella to serious Chianti, have this character. 'Black cherry' as a description is often used of Merlot wines – meaning they are sweet but have a firmness associated with the thicker skins of black cherries.

Cinsault – Black grape variety of southern France, where it is invariably blended with others in wines of all qualities ranging from vin de pays to the pricy reds of Châteauneuf du Pape. Also much-planted in South Africa. The effect in wine is to add keen aromas (sometimes compared with turpentine!) and softness to the blend. The name is often spelt Cinsaut.

Clape, La – A small *cru* (defined quality-vineyard area) within the Coteaux du Languedoc where the growers make some seriously delicious red wines, mainly from Carignan, Grenache and Syrah grapes. A name worth looking out for on labels from the region.

claret – The red wine of Bordeaux, France. It comes from

Latin *clarus,* meaning 'clear', recalling a time when the red wines of the region were much lighter in colour than they are now.

clarete – On Spanish labels indicates a pale-coloured red wine. *Tinto* signifies a deeper hue.

classed growth – English translation of French *cru classé* describes a group of 60 individual wine estates in the Médoc district of Bordeaux, which in 1855 were granted this new status on the basis that their wines were the most expensive at that time. The classification was a promotional wheeze to attract attention to the Bordeaux stand at that year's Great Exhibition in Paris. Amazingly, all of the 60 wines concerned are still in production and most still occupy more or less their original places in the pecking order price-wise. The league was divided up into five divisions from *Premier Grand Cru Classé* (just four wines originally, with one promoted in 1971 – the only change ever made to the classification) to *Cinquième Grand Cru Classé.* Other regions of Bordeaux, notably Graves and St Emilion, have since imitated Médoc and introduced their own rankings of *cru classé* estates.

classic – An overused term in every respect – wine descriptions being no exception. In this book, the word is used to describe a very good wine of its type. So, a 'classic' Cabernet Sauvignon is one that is recognisably and admirably characteristic of that grape.

Classico – Under Italy's wine laws, this word appended to the name of a DOC zone has an important significance. The *classico* wines of the region can only be made from vineyards lying in the best-rated areas, and wines thus labelled (e.g. Chianti Classico, Soave Classico, Valpolicella Classico) can be reliably counted on to be a cut above the rest.

Colombard – White grape variety of southern France. Once employed almost entirely for making the wine that is distilled for armagnac and cognac brandies, but lately restored to varietal prominence in the Vin de Pays des Côtes de Gascogne where high-tech wineries turn it into a fresh and crisp, if unchallenging, dry wine at a budget price. But beware, cheap Colombard (especially from South Africa) can still be very dull.

Conca de Barbera – Winemaking region of Catalonia, Spain.

co-op – Very many of France's good-quality, inexpensive wines are made by co-operatives. These are wine-producing factories whose members, and joint-owners, are local *vignerons* (vine-growers). Each year they sell their harvests to the co-op for turning into branded wines. In Italy, co-op wines can be identified by the words Cantina Sociale on the label and in Germany by the term *Winzergenossenschaft*.

Corbières – A name to look out for. It's an AC of France's Midi (deep south) and produces countless robust reds and a few interesting whites, often at bargain prices.

Cortese – Obscure white grape variety of Piedmont, Italy. At its best, makes amazingly delicious, keenly brisk and fascinating wines. Worth seeking out.

Costières de Nîmes – Until 1989, this AC of southern France was known as the Costières de Gard. It forms a buffer between the southern Rhône and Languedoc-Roussillon regions, and makes wines from broadly the same range of grape varieties. It's a name to look out for, the best red wines being notable for their concentration of colour and fruit, with the earthy-spiciness of the better Rhône wines and a likeable liquorice note. A few good white wines, too, and even a decent rosé or two.

Côte – In French, it simply means a side, or slope, of a hill. The implication in wine terms is that the grapes come from a vineyard ideally situated for maximum sunlight, good drainage and the unique soil conditions prevailing on the hill in question. It's fair enough to claim that vines grown on slopes might get more sunlight than those grown on the flat, but there is no guarantee whatsoever that any wine labelled 'Côtes du' this or that is made from grapes grown on a hillside anyway. Côtes du Rhône wines are a case in point. Many 'Côtes' wines come from entirely level vineyards and it is worth remembering that many of the vineyards of Bordeaux, producing most of the world's priciest wines, are little short of prairie-flat. The quality factor is determined much more significantly by the weather and the talents of the winemaker.

Côtes du Luberon – Appellation Contrôlée zone of Provence in south-east France. Wines, mostly red, are similar in style to Côtes du Rhône.

Côtes du Rhône – One of the biggest and best-known appellations of south-east France, covering an area roughly defined by the southern reaches of the valley of the River Rhône. Long notorious for cheap and execrable reds, the Côtes du Rhône AC has lately achieved remarkable improvements in quality at all points along the price scale. Lots of brilliant-value warm and spicy reds, principally from Grenache and Syrah grapes. There are also some white and rosé wines. Note that this region had a brilliant run of vintages up to 2001 but then a rain-and-storm-ruined one in 2002. Go for pre-2002 vintages if you have a choice.

Côtes du Rhône Villages – Appellation within the larger Côtes du Rhône AC for wine of supposed superiority made in a number of zones associated with a long list of nominated individual villages. *Villages* wines may be more interesting than their humbler counterparts, but this cannot be counted on. Go for the 2000 and 2001 vintages rather than 2002.

Côtes du Roussillon – Huge appellation of south-west France known for strong, dark, peppery reds often offering very decent value.

Côtes du Roussillon Villages – Appellation for superior wines from a number of nominated locations within the larger Roussillon AC. Some of these village wines can be of exceptional quality and value.

crianza – Means 'nursery' in Spanish. On Rioja and Navarra wines, the designation signifies a wine that has been nursed through a maturing period of at least a year in oak casks and a further six months in bottle before being released for sale.

cru – A word that crops up with confusing regularity on French wine labels. It means 'the growing' or 'the making' of a wine and asserts that the wine concerned is from a specific vineyard. Under the Appellation Contrôlée rules, countless *crus* are classified in various hierarchical ranks. Hundreds of individual vineyards are described as *premier cru* or *grand cru* in the classic wine regions of Alsace, Bordeaux, Burgundy and Champagne. The common denominator is that the wine can be counted on to be enormously expensive. On humbler wines, the use of the word *cru* tends to be mere decoration.

cru classé – *See* Classed growth.

cuve – A vat for wine, French.

cuvée – French for the wine in a *cuve,* or vat. The word is much used on labels to imply that the wine is from just one vat, and thus of unique, unblended character. *Premier cuvée* is supposedly the best wine from a given pressing because the grapes have had only the initial, gentle squashing to extract the free-run juice. Subsequent cuvées will have been from harsher pressings, grinding the grape pulp to extract the last drop of juice.

D

Dão – Major wine-producing region of northern Portugal now turning out much more interesting reds than it used to – worth looking out for anything made by mega-producer Sogrape.

demi sec – 'Half-dry' style of French (and some other) wines. Beware. It can mean anything from off-dry to cloyingly sweet.

DO – *Denominacion de Origen,* Spain's wine-regulating scheme, similar to France's AC, but older – the first DO region was Rioja, from 1926. DO wines are Spain's best, accounting for a third of the nation's annual production.

DOC – Stands for *Denominazione di Origine Controllata,* Italy's equivalent of France's AC. The wines are made according to the stipulations of each of its 280 denominated zones of origin, 20 of which enjoy the superior classification of DOCG (DOC with *e Garantita* – guaranteed – appended).

Durif – Rare black grape variety mostly of California, where it is also known as Petite Sirah, but with some plantings in Australia.

E

earthy – A tricky word in the wine vocabulary. In this book, its use is meant to be complimentary. It indicates that the wine somehow suggests the soil the grapes were grown in, even (perhaps a shade too poetically) the landscape in which the vineyards lie. The amazing-value red wines of the torrid, volcanic southernmost regions of Italy are often described as earthy. This is an association with the pleasantly 'scorched' back-flavour in wines made from the ultra-ripe harvests of this near-sub-tropical part of the world.

edge – A wine with edge is one with evident (although not excessive) acidity.

élevé – 'Brought up' in French. Much used on wine labels where the wine has been matured (brought up) in oak barrels *élevé en fûts de chêne* to give it extra dimensions.

Entre Deux Mers – Meaning 'between two seas', it's a region lying between the Dordogne and Garonne rivers of Bordeaux, now mainly known for dry white wines from Sauvignon and Semillon grapes. Quality rarely seems exciting.

Estremadura – Wine-producing region occupying Portugal's coastal area north of Lisbon. Lots of interesting wines from indigenous grape varieties, usually at bargain prices. If a label mentions Estremadura, it is a safe rule that there might be something good within.

F

Faugères – AC of the Languedoc in south-west France. Source of many hearty, economic reds.

Feteasca – White grape variety widely grown in Romania. Name means 'maiden's grape' and the wine tends to be soft and slightly sweet.

Fiano – White grape variety of Sicily, lately revived. It is said to have been cultivated by the ancient Romans for a wine called Apianum.

finish – The last flavour lingering in the mouth after wine has been swallowed.

fino – Pale and very dry style of sherry. You drink it thoroughly chilled – and you don't keep it any longer after opening than other dry white wines. Needs to be fresh to be at its best.

Fitou – One of the first 'designer' wines, it's an appellation in France's Languedoc region, where production is dominated by one huge co-operative, the Vignerons de Mont Tauch. Back in the 1970s, this co-op paid a corporate-image company to come up with a Fitou logo and label-design style, and the wines have prospered ever since. And it's not just packaging – Fitou at all price levels can be very good value, especially from the Mont Tauch co-op.

flabby – Fun word describing a wine that tastes dilute or watery, with insufficient acidity.

flying winemaker – Back-labels on supermarket wines sometimes boast that the contents are made by a flying winemaker. They're consultants who visit vineyards worldwide at harvest time to oversee the production process, perhaps to ensure that the style of wine wanted by a major customer (usually a supermarket) is adhered to by the locals. These people are very often Australian, with degrees in oenology (the science of winemaking) and well up on latest technology and biochemistry. If there is a criticism of flying winemakers, it is that they have a tendency to impose a uniform style on all the vineyards upon which they descend. Thus, more and more French, Italian and Spanish wines, for example, are starting to take on the 'upfront fruitiness' of the wines of Australia.

fruit – In tasting terms, the fruit is the greater part of the overall flavour of a wine. The wine is (or should be) after all, composed entirely of fruit.

G

Gamay – The black grape that makes all red Beaujolais. It is a pretty safe rule to avoid Gamay wines from any other region. It's a grape that does not do well elsewhere.

Garganega – White grape variety of the Veneto region of north-west Italy. Best known as the principal ingredient of Soave, but occasionally included in varietal blends and mentioned as such on labels. Correctly pronounced 'gar-GAN-iga'.

Garnacha – Spanish black grape variety synonymous with Grenache of France. It is blended with Tempranillo to make the red wines of Rioja and Navarra, and is now quite widely cultivated elsewhere in Spain to make grippingly fruity varietals.

Gavi – DOC for dry but rich white wine from Cortese grapes in Piedmont, north-east Italy. Trendy Gavi di Gavi wines tend to be enjoyably lush, but are rather expensive.

Gewürztraminer – One of the great grape varieties of Alsace, France. At their best, the wines are perfumed with lychees and are richly, spicily fruity, yet quite dry. Gewürztraminer from Alsace is almost always expensive – never under £5 – but the grape is also grown with some success in Eastern Europe, Germany, Italy and South America, and sold at more approachable prices. Pronounced 'geh-VOORTS-traminner'.

Graciano – Black grape variety of Spain that is one of the minor constituents of Rioja. Better known in its own right in

Australia where it can make dense, spicy, long-lived red wines.

green – In flavour, a wine that is unripe and raw-tasting.

Grenache – The mainstay of the wines of the southern Rhône Valley in France. Grenache is usually the greater part of the mix in Côtes du Rhône reds and is widely planted right across the neighbouring Languedoc-Roussillon region. It's a big-cropping variety that thrives even in the hottest climates and is really a blending grape – most commonly with Syrah, the noble variety of the northern Rhône. Few French wines are labelled with its name, but the grape has caught on in Australia in a big way and it is now becoming a familiar varietal, known for strong, dark liquorous reds. Grenache is the French name for what is originally a Spanish variety, Garnacha.

grip – In wine-tasting terminology, the sensation in the mouth produced by a wine that has a healthy quantity of tannin in it. A wine with grip is a good wine. A wine with too much tannin, or which is still too young (the tannin hasn't 'softened' with age) is not described as having grip, but as mouth-puckering – or simply undrinkable.

Grüner Veltliner – The 'national' white-wine grape of Austria. In the past it made mostly soft, German-style everyday wines, but now is behind some excellent dry styles, too.

H

halbtrocken – 'Half-dry' in Germany's wine vocabulary. A reassurance that the wine is not some ghastly sugared Liebfraumilch-style confection.

hock – The wine of Germany's Rhine river valleys. It comes in brown bottles, as distinct from the wine of the Mosel river valleys – which comes in green ones.

I

Indicazione Geografica Tipica – Italy's recently instituted wine-quality designation, broadly equivalent to France's *vin de pays*. The label has to state the geographical location of the vineyard and will often (but not always) state the principal grape varieties from which the wine is made.

Inycon – A recent wine brand of Sicily's huge Settesoli co-operative and the label on several wines mentioned in this book. *Inycon* was the Ancient Greek name of the modern Sicilian village of Menfi where the vineyards and winery for the brand have been established.

J

jammy – the 'sweetness' in dry red wines is supposed to evoke ripeness rather than sugariness. Sometimes, flavours include a sweetness reminiscent of jam. Usually a fault in the winemaking technique.

joven – Young wine, Spanish. In regions such as Rioja, *vino joven* is a synonym for *sin crianza,* which means 'without ageing' in cask or bottle.

K

Kabinett – Under Germany's bewildering wine-quality rules, this is a classification of a top-quality (QmP) wine. Expect a keen, dry, racy style. The name comes from the cabinet or cupboard in which winemakers traditionally kept their most treasured bottles.

Kekfrankos – Black grape variety of Hungary, particularly the Sopron region, which makes some of the country's more interesting red wines, characterised by colour and spiciness. Same variety as Austria's Blaufrankisch.

L

Lambrusco The name is that of a black grape variety widely grown across northern Italy. True Lambrusco wine is red, dry and very slightly sparkling, but from the 1980s Britain has been deluged with a strange, sweet manifestation of the style, which has done little to enhance the good name of the original. Good Lambrusco is delicious and fun.

Languedoc-Roussillon – Vast area of southern France, including the country's south-west Mediterranean region. The source, now, of many great-value wines from countless ACs and vin de pays zones.

legs – The liquid residue left clinging to the sides of the glass after wine has been swirled. The persistence of the legs is an indicator of the weight of alcohol. Also known as 'tears'.

liquorice – The pungent slightly burnt flavours of this once-fashionable confection are detectable in some wines made from very ripe grapes, for example, the Malbec harvested in Argentina and several varieties grown in the very hot vineyards of southernmost Italy. A close synonym is 'tarry'. This characteristic is by no means a fault in red wine, unless very dominant, but it can make for a challenging flavour that might not appeal to all tastes.

liquorous – Wines of great weight and glyceriney texture (evidenced by the 'legs', or 'tears', which cling to the glass after the wine has been swirled) are always noteworthy. The connection with liquor is drawn in respect of the feel of the wine in the mouth, rather than with the higher alcoholic strength of spirits.

Lugana – DOC of Lombardy, Italy known for a dry white wine that is often of real distinction – rich, almondy stuff from the ubiquitous Trebbiano grape.

M

Macabeo – One of the main grapes used for *cava*, the sparkling wine of Spain. It is the same grape as Viura.

Mâcon – Town and collective appellation of southern Burgundy, France. Lightweight white wines from Chardonnay grapes and similarly light reds from Pinot Noir and some Gamay. The better ones, and the ones exported, have the AC Mâcon-Villages and there are individual-village wines with their own ACs including Mâcon-Clessé, Mâcon-Viré and Mâcon-Lugny.

Malbec – Black grape variety grown on a small scale in Bordeaux, and the mainstay of the wines of Cahors in France's Dordogne region under the name Cot. Now much better known for producing big butch reds in Argentina.

Mantinia – Winemaking region of the Peloponnese, Greece. Dry whites from Moschofilero grapes are aromatic and refreshing.

Manzanilla – Pale, very dry sherry of Sanlucar de Barrameida, a grungy seaport on the southernmost coast of Spain. Manzanilla is proud to be distinct from the pale, very dry fino sherry of the main producing town of Jerez de la Frontera down the coast. Drink it chilled and fresh – it goes downhill in an opened bottle after just a few days, even if kept (as it should be) in the fridge.

Margaret River – Vineyard region of Western Australia regarded as ideal for grape varieties including Cabernet Sauvignon. It is has a relatively cool climate and a reputation for making sophisticated wines, both red and white.

Marlborough – Best-known vineyard region of New Zealand's South Island has a cool climate and a name for brisk but cerebral Sauvignon Blanc and Chardonnay wines.

Marsanne – White grape variety of the northern Rhône Valley and, increasingly, of the wider south of France. It's known for making well-coloured wines with heady aroma and fruit.

Mataro – Black grape variety of Australia. It's the same as the Mourvèdre of France and Monastrell of Spain.

McLaren Vale – Vineyard region south of Adelaide in south-east Australia. Known for serious-quality wines from grape varieties including Shiraz and Chardonnay.

meaty – Weighty, rich red wine style.

Mendoza – The region to watch in Argentina. Lying to the east of the Andes mountains, just about opposite the best vineyards of Chile on the other side, Mendoza accounts for the bulk of Argentine wine production, with quality improving fast.

Merlot – One of the great black wine grapes of Bordeaux, and now grown all over the world. The name is said to derive from the French *merle,* meaning a blackbird. Characteristics of Merlot-based wines attract descriptions such as 'plummy' and 'plump' with black-cherry aroma. The grapes are larger than most, and thus have less skin in proportion to their flesh. This means the resulting wines have less tannin than wines from smaller-berry varieties such as Cabernet Sauvignon, and are therefore, in the Bordeaux context at least, more suitable for drinking while still relatively young.

middle palate – In wine-tasting, the impression given by the wine when it is held in the mouth.

Midi – Catch-all term for the deep south of France west of the Rhône Valley.

mineral – Good dry white wines can have a crispness and freshness that somehow evokes this word. Purity of flavour is a key.

Minervois – AC for (mostly) red wines from vineyards around the town of Minerve in the Languedoc-Roussillon region of France. Often good value.

Monastrell – Black grape variety of Spain, widely planted in Mediterranean regions for inexpensive wines notable for their high alcohol and toughness – though they can mature into excellent, soft reds. The variety is known in France as Mourvèdre and in Australia as Mataro.

Monbazillac – AC for sweet, dessert wines within the wider appellation of Bergerac in south-west France. Made from the same grape varieties (principally Sauvignon and Semillon) that go into the much costlier counterpart wines of Barsac and Sauternes near Bordeaux, these stickies from botrytis-affected, late-harvested grapes can be delicious and good value for money.

Montalcino – Hill town of Tuscany, Italy, and a DOCG for strong and very long-lived red wines from Brunello grapes. The wines are mostly very expensive. Rosso di Montalcino, a DOC for the humbler wines of the zone, is often a good buy.

Montepulciano – Black grape variety of Italy. Best-known in Montepulciano d'Abruzzo, the juicy, purply-black and bramble-fruited red of the Abruzzi region mid-way down Italy's Adriatic side. Also the grape in the rightly popular hearty reds of Rosso Conero from around Ancona in the Marches. Not to be confused with the hill town of Montepulciano in Tuscany, famous for expensive Vino Nobile di Montepulciano wine.

morello – Lots of red wines have smells and flavours redolent of cherries. Morello cherries, among the darkest-coloured and sweetest of all varieties and the preferred choice of cherry-brandy producers, have a distinct sweetness resembled by some wines made from Merlot grapes. A morello whiff or taste is generally very welcome.

Moscatel – Spanish Muscat.

Moscato – *See* Muscat.

Moselle – The wine of Germany's Mosel river valleys, collectively known for winemaking purposes as Mosel-Saar-Ruwer. The wine always comes in slim, green bottles, as distinct from the brown bottles employed for Rhine wines.

Mourvèdre – Widely planted black grape variety of southern France. It's an ingredient in many of the wines of Provence, the Rhône and Languedoc, including the ubiquitous Vin de Pays d'Oc. It's a hot-climate vine and the wine is usually blended with other varieties to give sweet aromas and 'backbone' to the mix. Known as Mataro in Australia and Monastrell in Spain.

Muscadet – One of France's most familiar everyday whites. It comes from vineyards at the estuarial end of the river Loire, and at its best has something of a sea-breezy freshness about it. The better wines are reckoned to be those from the vineyards in the Sèvre et Maine region, and many are made *sur lie* – 'on the lees' – meaning that the wine is left in contact with the yeasty deposit of its fermentation until just before bottling, in an endeavour to add interest to what can sometimes be an acidic and fruitless style.

Muscat – Grape variety with origins in ancient Greece, and still grown widely among the Aegean islands for the production of sweet white wines. Muscats are the wines that taste more like grape-juice than any other – but the high sugar levels ensure they are also among the most alcoholic of wines, too. Known as Moscato in Italy, the grape is much used for making sweet sparkling wines, as in Asti Spumante or Moscato d'Asti. There are several appellations in south-west France for inexpensive Muscats made rather like port, part-fermented before the addition of grape alcohol to halt the conversion of sugar into alcohol, creating a sweet and heady *vin doux naturel*. Dry Muscat wines, when well made, have a delicious sweet aroma but a refreshing, light touch with flavours reminiscent variously of orange blossom, wood smoke and grapefruit.

must – New-pressed grape juice prior to fermentation.

N

Navarra – DO wine-producing region of northern Spain adjacent to, and overshadowed by, Rioja. Navarra's wines can be startlingly akin to their neighbouring rivals, and sometimes rather better value for money.

négociant – In France, a dealer-producer who buys wines from growers and matures and/or blends them for sale under his own label. Purists can be a bit sniffy about these entrepreneurs, claiming that only the vine-grower with his or her own winemaking set-up can make truly authentic stuff, but the truth is that many of the best wines of France are négociant-produced – especially at the humbler end of the price scale. Négociants are often identified on wine labels as *négociant-éleveur* (literally 'dealer-bringer-up') and meaning that the wine has been matured, blended and bottled by the party in question.

Negro Amaro – Black grape variety mainly of Apulia, the fast-improving wine region of south-east Italy. Dense, earthy red wines with ageing potential and plenty of alcohol. The grape behind Copertino.

Nero d'Avola – Black grape variety of Sicily and southern Italy. It makes deep-coloured wines that, given half a chance, can develop intensity and richness with age.

non-vintage – A wine is described as such when it has been blended from the harvests of more than one year. A non-vintage wine is not necessarily an inferior one, but under quality-control regulations around the world, still table wines most usually derive solely from one year's grape crop to qualify for appellation status. Champagnes and sparkling wines are mostly blended from several vintages, as are fortified wines, such as basic port and sherry.

nose – In the vocabulary of the wine-taster, the nose is the scent of a wine. Sounds a bit dotty, but it makes a sensible-enough alternative to the rather bald 'smell'. The use of the word 'perfume' implies that the wine smells particularly good. 'Aroma' is used specifically to describe a wine that smells as it should, as in 'this Burgundy has the authentic strawberry-raspberry aroma of Pinot Noir'.

O

oak – Most of the world's most-expensive wines are matured in new or nearly new oak barrels, giving additional opulence of flavour. Of late, many cheaper wines have been getting the oak treatment, too, in older, cheaper casks, or simply by having sacks of oak chippings poured into their steel or fibreglass holding tanks. 'Oak aged' on a label is likely to indicate the latter treatments. But the overtly oaked wines of Australia have in some cases been so overdone, there is now a reactive trend whereby some producers proclaim their wines – particularly Chardonnays – as 'unoaked' on the label, thereby asserting that the flavours are more naturally achieved.

Oltrepo Pavese – Wine-producing zone of Piedmont, north-west Italy. The name means 'south of Pavia across the [river] Po' and the wines, both white and red, can be excellent quality and value for money.

organic wine – As in other sectors of the food industry, demand for organically made wine is – or appears to be – growing. As a rule, a wine qualifies as organic if it comes entirely from grapes grown in vineyards cultivated without the use of synthetic materials, and made in a winery where chemical treatments or additives are shunned with similar vigour. In fact, there are plenty of winemakers in the world using organic methods, but who disdain to label their bottles as such. Wines that do brazenly proclaim their organic status tend to carry the same sort of premium as their counterparts round the corner in the fruit, vegetable and meat aisles. The upshot is that there is only a limited choice of lower-priced organic wine. There is no single worldwide (or even Europe-wide) standard for organic food or wine, so you pretty much have to take the producer's word for it.

P

Pasqua – One of the biggest and, it should be said, best wine producers of the Veneto region of north-west Italy.

Passetoutgrains – *Bourgogne passetoutgrains* is a generic appellation of the Burgundy region, France. The word loosely means 'any grapes allowed' and is supposed specifically to designate a red wine made with Gamay grapes as well as

Burgundy's principal black variety, Pinot Noir, in a ratio of two parts Gamay to one of Pinot. The wine is usually relatively inexpensive, and relatively uninteresting, too.

Periquita – Black grape variety of southern Portugal. Makes rather exotic spicy reds. Name means 'parrot'.

Petite Sirah – Black grape variety of California and Latin America known for plenty of colour and long life. Not related to the Syrah of the Rhône.

Petit Verdot – Black grape variety of Bordeaux used to give additional colour, density and spiciness to Cabernet Sauvignon-dominated blends. Strictly a minority player at home, but in Australia and California it is grown as the principal variety for some big hearty reds of real character.

petrol – When white wines from certain grapes, especially Riesling, are allowed to age in the bottle for longer than a year or two, they can take on a spirity aroma reminiscent of petrol or diesel. In grand mature German wines, this is considered a very good thing.

Picpoul de Pinet – Obscure white grape variety of the southern Rhône region of France that occasionally makes interesting floral dry whites.

Piemonte – North-western province of Italy, which we call Piedmont, known for the spumante wines of the town of Asti, plus expensive Barbaresco and Barolo and better-value varietal red wines from Barbera and Dolcetto grapes.

Pinotage – South Africa's own black grape variety. Makes red wines ranging from light and juicy to dark, strong and long-lived. It's a cross between Pinot Noir and a grape the South Africans used to call Hermitage (thus the portmanteau name) but turns out to have been Cinsault. Cheaper Pinotages tend to disappoint, but there has been an improvement of late in the standard of some wines tasted.

Pinot Blanc – White grape variety principally of Alsace, France. Florally perfumed, exotically fruity dry white wines.

Pinot Grigio – White grape variety of northern Italy. Wines bearing its name have become fashionable in recent times. Good examples have an interesting smoky-pungent aroma and keen, slaking fruit. But most are dull. Originally a French grape, there known as Pinot Gris, which is renowned for making lushly exotic – and expensive – white wines in the Alsace region.

Pinot Noir – The great black grape of Burgundy, France. It makes all the region's fabulously expensive red wines. Notoriously difficult to grow in warmer climates, it is nevertheless cultivated by countless intrepid winemakers in the New World intent on reproducing the magic appeal of red Burgundy. California and New Zealand have come closest, but rarely at prices much below those for the real thing. Some Chilean Pinot Noirs (Cono Sur, for example) are inexpensive and worth trying.

Pouilly Fuissé – Village and AC of the Mâconnais region of southern Burgundy in France. Dry white wines from Chardonnay grapes. Wines are among the highest-rated of the Mâconnais.

Pouilly Fumé – Village and AC of the Loire Valley in France. Dry white wines from Sauvignon Blanc grapes. Similar 'pebbly', 'grassy' or even 'gooseberry' style to neighbouring AC Sancerre. The notion put about by some enthusiasts that Pouilly Fumé is 'smoky' is surely nothing more than word-association with the name.

Primitivo – Black grape variety of southern Italy, especially the region of Apulia/Puglia. The wines are typically dense and dark in colour with plenty of alcohol, and have an earthy, spicy style. Often a real bargain. It is believed to be closely related to California's Zinfandel, which makes purple, brambly wines of a very different hue.

Prosecco – White grape variety of Italy's Veneto region which gives its name to a light, sparkling and cheap wine that is much appreciated locally, but not widely exported.

Puglia – The region occupying the 'heel' of southern Italy, and one of the world's fastest-improving sources of inexpensive wines. Modern winemaking techniques and large regional grants from the EU are at least partly responsible.

Q

QbA – German, standing for *Qualitätswein bestimmter Anbaugebiet*. It means 'quality wine from designated areas' and implies that the wine is made from grapes with a minimum level of ripeness, but it's by no means a guarantee of exciting quality. Only wines labelled QmP (see next entry) can be depended upon to be special.

QmP – Stands for *Qualitätswein mit Prädikat*. These are the serious wines of Germany, made without the addition of sugar to 'improve' them. To qualify for QmP status, the grapes must reach a level of ripeness as measured on a sweetness scale – all according to Germany's fiendishly complicated wine-quality regulations. Wines from grapes that reach the stated minimum level of sweetness qualify for the description of *Kabinett*. The next level up earns the rank of *Spätlese,* meaning 'late-picked'. Kabinett wines can be expected to be dry and brisk in style, and Spätlese wines a little bit riper and fuller. The next grade up, *Auslese,* meaning 'selected harvest', indicates a wine made from super-ripe grapes; it will be golden in colour and honeyed in flavour. A generation ago, these wines were as valued, and as expensive, as any of the world's grandest appellations, but the collapse in demand for German wines in the UK – brought about by the disrepute rightly earned for floods of filthy Liebfraumilch – means they are now seriously undervalued.

Quincy – AC of Loire Valley, France, known for pebbly-dry white wines from Sauvignon grapes. The wines are forever compared to those of nearby and much better-known Sancerre – and Quincy often represents better value for money. Pronounced 'KAN-see'.

Quinta – Portuguese for farm or estate. It precedes the names of many of Portugal's best-known wines. It is pronounced 'KEEN-ta'.

R

racy – Evocative wine-tasting description for wine that thrills the tastebuds with a rush of exciting sensations. Good Rieslings often qualify.

raisiny – Wines from grapes that have been very ripe or overripe at harvest can take on a smell and flavour akin to the concentrated, heat-dried sweetness of raisins. As a minor element in the character of a wine, this can add to the appeal but as a dominant characteristic it is a fault.

rancio – Spanish term harking back to Roman times when wines were commonly stored in jars outside, exposed to the sun, so they oxidised and took on a burnt sort of flavour. Today, rancio describes a baked – and by no means unpleasant – flavour in fortified wines, particularly sherry and Madeira.

Reserva – In Portugal and Spain, this has genuine significance. The Portuguese use it for special wines with a higher alcohol level and longer ageing, although the precise periods vary between regions. In Spain, especially in the Navarra and Rioja regions, it means the wine must have had at least a year in oak and two in bottle before release.

reserve – On French (as *réserve*) or other wines, this implies special-quality, longer-aged wines, but has no official significance.

Retsina – The universal white wine of Greece. It has been traditionally made in Attica, the region of Athens, for a very long time, and is said to owe its origins and name to the ancient custom of sealing *amphorae* (terracotta jars) of the wine with a gum made from pine resin. Some of the flavour of the resin inevitably transmitted itself into the wine, and ancient Greeks acquired a lasting taste for it.

Reuilly – AC of Loire Valley, France, for crisp dry whites from Sauvignon grapes. Pronounced 'RUR-yee'.

Ribatejo – Emerging wine region of Portugal. Worth seeking out on labels of red wines in particular, because new winemakers are producing lively stuff from distinctive indigenous grapes such as Castelao and Trincadeira.

Ribera del Duero – Classic wine region of north-west Spain lying along the river Duero (which crosses the border to become Portugal's Douro, forming the valley where port comes from). It is the home to an estate rather oddly named Vega Sicilia, where red wines of epic quality are made and sold at equally epic prices. Further down the scale, some very good reds are made, too.

Riesling – The noble grape variety of Germany. It is correctly pronounced 'REEZ-ling', not 'RICE-ling'. Once notorious as the grape behind all those boring 'medium' Liebfraumilches and Niersteiners, this grape has had a bad press. In fact, there has never been much, if any, Riesling in Germany's cheap-and-nasty plonks. But the country's best wines, the so-called *Qualitätswein mit Prädikat* grades, are made almost exclusively with Riesling. These wines range from crisply fresh and appley styles to extravagantly fruity, honeyed wines from late-harvested grapes. Excellent Riesling wines are also made in Alsace and now in Australia.

Rioja – The principal fine-wine region of Spain, in the country's north east. The pricier wines are noted for their vanilla-pod richness from long ageing in oak casks. Younger wines, labelled variously *joven* (young) and *sin-crianza* (meaning they are without barrel-ageing), are cheaper and can make relishable drinking.

Ripasso – A particular style of Valpolicella wine. New wine is partially refermented in vats that have been used to make the *recioto* reds (wines made from semi-dried grapes), thus creating a bigger, smoother (and more alcoholic) version of usually-light and pale Valpolicella.

Riserva – In Italy, a wine made only in the best vintages, and allowed longer ageing in cask and bottle.

Rivaner – Alternative name for Germany's Müller-Thurgau grape, the life-blood of Liebfraumilch.

Riverland – Vineyard region to the immediate north of the Barossa Valley of South Australia, extending east into New South Wales.

rosso – Red wine, Italy.

Rosso Conero – DOC red wine made in the environs of Ancona in the Marches, Italy. Made from the Montepulciano grape, the wine can provide excellent value for money.

Ruby Cabernet – Black grape variety of California, created by crossing Cabernet Sauvignon and Carignan. Makes soft and squelchy red wine at home and in South Africa.

Rueda – DO of north-west Spain making first-class refreshing dry whites from the indigenous Verdejo grape, imported Sauvignon grape, and others. Exciting quality – and prices, so far, are keen.

Rully – AC of Chalonnais region of southern Burgundy, France. White wines from Chardonnay and red wines from Pinot Noir grapes. Both can be very good and are substantially cheaper than their more northerly Burgundian neighbours. Pronounced 'ROO-yee'.

S

Salento – Up and coming wine region of southern Italy. Many good bargain reds from local grapes including Nero d'Avola and Primitivo.

Sancerre – AC of the Loire Valley, France, renowned for flinty-fresh Sauvignon whites and rarer Pinot Noir reds. These wines are never cheap, and recent tastings make it plain that only the best-made, individual-producer wines are worth the money. Budget brands seem mostly dull.

Sangiovese – The local black grape of Tuscany, Italy. It is the principal variety used for Chianti and is now widely planted in Latin America – often making delicious, Chianti-like wines with characteristic cherryish-but-deeply-ripe fruit and a dry, clean finish. Chianti wines have become (unjustifiably) expensive in recent years and cheaper Italian wines such as those called Sangiovese di Toscana make a consoling substitute.

Santorini – Island of Greece's Cyclades was the site in about 1500BC of a tremendous volcanic explosion. The huge caldera of the volcano – a circular mini-archipelago – is now planted with vines producing very trendy and likeable dry white wines at fair prices.

Saumur – Town and appellation of Loire Valley, France. Characterful minerally red wines from Cabernet Franc grapes, and some whites. The once-popular sparkling wines from Chenin Blanc grapes are now little seen in Britain.

Saumur-Champigny – Separate appellation for red wines from Cabernet Franc grapes of Saumur in the Loire, sometimes very good and lively.

Sauvignon Blanc – French white grape variety now grown worldwide. The wines are characterised by aromas of gooseberry, fresh-cut grass, even asparagus. Flavours are often described as 'grassy' or 'nettley'.

sec – Dry wine style. French.

secco – Dry wine style. Italian.

Semillon – White grape variety originally of Bordeaux, where it is blended with Sauvignon Blanc to make fresh dry whites and, when harvested very late in the season, the ambrosial sweet whites of Barsac, Sauternes and other appellations. Even in the driest wines, the grape can be recognised from its honeyed, sweet-pineapple, even banana-like aromas. Now widely planted in Australia and Latin America, and frequently blended with Chardonnay to make interesting dry whites.

sherry – The great aperitif wine of Spain, centred on the Andalusian city of Jerez (from which the name 'sherry' is an English mispronunciation). There is a lot of sherry-style wine in the world, but only the authentic wine from Jerez and the neighbouring producing towns of Puerta de Santa Maria and Sanlucar de Barrameida may label their wines as such. The Spanish drink real sherry – very dry and fresh, pale in colour and served well-chilled – called *fino* and *manzanilla,* and darker but naturally dry variations called *amontillado, palo cortado* and *oloroso.* The stuff sold under the big brand names for the British market are sweetened, coloured commercial yuck for putting in trifles or sideboard decanters to gather dust. The sherries recommended in this book are all real wines, made the way the Spanish like them.

Shiraz – Australian name for the Syrah grape. Aussie Shirazes, unlike their silky-spicy southern-French counterparts, tend to be big, muscular and alcoholic wines with earthy darkness.

Sogrape – The leading wine company of Portugal, which built its fortune on Mateus Rosé. Sogrape is based in the Douro region, where port comes from, and makes many excellent table wines both locally and further afield. In 2002, Sogrape added the huge port (and sherry) house of Sandeman to its port-making interests.

Somontano – Wine region of north-east Spain. Name means 'under the mountains' – in this case the Pyrenees – and the region has had DO status only since 1984. Much innovative winemaking here, with New World styles emerging. Some very good buys. A region to watch.

souple – French wine-tasting term that translates into English as 'supple' or even 'docile' as in 'pliable' but I understand it in the vinous context to mean muscular but soft – a wine with tannin as well as soft fruit.

Spätlese – *See* QmP.

spirity – Some wines, mostly from the New World, are made from grapes so ripe at harvest that their high alcohol content can be detected through a mildly burning sensation on the tongue, similar to the effect of sipping a spirit.

spritzy – Describes a wine with a barely detectable sparkle. Some young wines are intended to have this elusive fizziness; in others it is a fault.

spumante – Sparkling wine of Italy. Asti Spumante is the best known, from the town of Asti in the north-west Italian province of Piemonte. The term describes wines that are fully sparkling. *Frizzante* wines have a less vigorous mousse.

stalky – A useful tasting term to describe red wines with flavours that make you think the stalks from the grape bunches must have been fermented along with the must (juice). Young Bordeaux reds very often have this mild astringency. In moderation it's fine, but if it dominates it probably signifies the wine is at best immature and at worst badly made.

Stellenbosch – Town and region at the heart of South Africa's burgeoning wine industry. It's an hour's drive from Cape Town and the source of much of the country's cheaper wine. Quality is variable, and the name Stellenbosch on a label can't (yet, anyway) be taken as a guarantee of quality.

stony – Wine-tasting term for keenly dry white wines. It's meant to indicate a wine of purity and real quality, with just the right match of fruit and acidity.

structured – Good wines are not one-dimensional, they have layers of flavour and texture. A structured wine has phases of enjoyment: the 'attack' or first impression in the mouth; the middle palate as the wine is held in the mouth; the lingering aftertaste.

summer fruit – Wine-tasting term intended to convey a smell or taste of soft fruits such as strawberries and raspberries – without having to commit too specifically to which.

Superiore – On labels of Italian wines, this is more than an idle boast. Under DOC rules, wines must qualify for the *superiore* designation by reaching one or more specified quality levels, usually a higher alcohol content or an additional period of maturation. Frascati, for example, qualifies for DOC status at 11.5 per cent alcohol, but to be classified *superiore* must have 12 per cent alcohol.

sur lie – Literally, 'on the lees'. It's a term now widely used on the labels of Muscadet wines, signifying that after fermentation has died down, the new wine has been left in the tank over the winter on the lees – the detritus of yeasts and other interesting compounds left over from the turbid fermentation process. The idea is that additional interest is imparted into the flavour of the wine.

Syrah – The noble grape of the Rhône Valley, France. Makes very dark, dense wine characterised by peppery, tarry aromas. Now planted all over southern France and farther afield. In Australia, where it makes wines ranging from disagreeably jam-like plonks to wonderfully rich and silky keeping wines, it is known as Shiraz.

T

table wine – Wine that is unfortified and of an alcoholic strength, for UK tax purposes anyway, of no more than 15 per cent. I use the term to distinguish, for example, between the red table wines of the Douro Valley in Portugal and the region's better-known fortified wine, port.

Tafelwein – Table wine, German. The humblest quality designation, which doesn't usually bode very well.

tank method – Bulk-production process for sparkling wines. Base wine undergoes secondary fermentation in a large, sealed vat rather than in individual closed bottles. Also known as the Charmat method after the name of the inventor of the process.

tannin – Well-known as the film-forming, teeth-coating component in tea, tannin is a natural compound occurring in black grape skins and acts as a natural preservative in wine. Its noticeable presence in wine is regarded as a good thing. It gives young everyday reds their dryness, firmness of flavour and backbone. And it helps high-quality reds to retain their lively fruitiness for many years. A grand Bordeaux red when first made, for example, will have purply-sweet, rich fruit and mouth-puckering tannin, but after ten years or so this will have evolved into a delectably fruity mature wine in which the formerly parching effects of the tannin have receded almost completely, leaving the shade of 'residual tannin' that marks out a great wine approaching maturity.

tarry – On the whole, winemakers don't like critics to say their wines evoke the redolence of road repairs, but I can't helping using this term to describe the agreeable, sweet, 'burnt' flavour that is often found at the centre of the fruit in wines from Argentina, Italy and Portugal in particular.

TCA – Dread ailment in wine caused by faulty corks. It stands for 246 trichloroanisol and is characterised by a horrible musty smell and flavour in the affected wine. It is largely because of the current plague of TCA that so many wine producers worldwide are now going over to polymer 'corks' and screwcaps.

tears – The colourless alcohol in the wine left clinging to the inside of the glass after the contents have been swirled. Persistent tears (also known as 'legs') indicate a wine of good concentration.

Tempranillo – The great black grape of Spain. Along with Garnacha (Grenache in France) it makes all red Rioja and Navarra wines and, under many pseudonyms, is an important or exclusive contributor to the wines of many other regions of Spain. It is also widely cultivated in South America.

tinto – On Spanish labels indicates a deeply coloured red wine. *Clarete* denotes a paler colour. Also Portuguese.

Toro – Quality wine region east of Zamora, Spain.

Torrontes – White grape variety of Argentina. Makes soft, dry wines often with delicious grapey-spicy aroma, similar in style to the classic dry Muscat wines of Alsace, but at more accessible prices.

Touraine – Region encompassing a swathe of the Loire Valley, France. Non-AC wines may be labelled 'Sauvignon de Touraine' etc.

Traminer – Grape variety, the same as Gewürztraminer.

Trebbiano – The workhorse white grape of Italy. A productive variety that is easy to cultivate, it seems to be included in just about every ordinary white wine of the entire nation – including Frascati, Orvieto and Soave. It is the same grape as France's Ugni Blanc.

Trincadeira Preta – Portuguese black grape variety native to the port-producing vineyards of the Douro Valley (where it goes under the name Tinta Amarella). In southern Portugal, it produces dark and sturdy table wines.

trocken – 'Dry' German wine. It's a recent trend among commercial-scale producers in the Rhine and Mosel to label their wines with this description in the hope of reassuring consumers that the contents do not resemble the dreaded sugar-water Liebfraumilch-type plonks of the bad old days. But the description does have a particular meaning under German wine law, namely that there is only a low level of unfermented sugar lingering in the wine (9 grams per litre, if you need to know), and this can leave the wine tasting rather austere.

U

Ugni Blanc – The most widely cultivated white grape variety of France and the mainstay of many a cheap dry white wine. To date it has been better known as the provider of base wine for distilling into Armagnac and Cognac, but lately the name has been appearing on wine labels. Technology seems to be improving the performance of the grape. The curious name is pronounced 'OON-yee', and is the same variety as Italy's ubiquitous Trebbiano.

V

Vacqueyras – Village of the southern Rhône valley of France in the region better known for its generic appellation, the Côtes du Rhône. Vacqueyras can date its winemaking history all the way back to 1414, but has only been producing under its own village AC since 1991. The wines, from Grenache and Syrah grapes, can be wonderfully silky and intense, spicy and long-lived.

Valdepeñas – An island of quality-production amidst the ocean of mediocrity that is Spain's La Mancha region – where most of the grapes are grown for distilling into the head-banging brandies of Jerez. Valdepeñas reds are made from a grape they call the Cencibel – which turns out to be a very close relation of the Tempranillo grape that is the mainstay of the fine but expensive red wines of Rioja. Again, like Rioja, Valdepeñas wines are matured in oak casks to give them a vanilla-rich smoothness. Among bargain reds, Valdepeñas is a name to look out for.

Valpolicella – Red wine of Verona, Italy. Good examples have ripe, cherry fruit and a pleasingly dry finish. Unfortunately, there are many bad examples of Valpolicella. Shop with circumspection. Valpolicella Classico wines, from the best vineyards clustered around the town, are more reliable. Those additionally labelled *superiore* have higher alcohol and some bottle-age.

vanilla – Ageing wines in oak barrels (or, less picturesquely, adding oak chips to wine in huge concrete vats) imparts a range of characteristics including a smell of vanilla from the ethyl vanilline naturally given off by oak.

varietal – A varietal wine is one named after the grape variety (one or more) from which it is made. Nearly all everyday wines worldwide are now labelled in this way. It is salutary to contemplate that just 20 years ago, wines described thus were virtually unknown outside Germany and one or two quirky regions of France and Italy.

vegan-friendly – My informal way of noting that a wine is claimed to have been made not only with animal-products-free finings (see Vegetarian wine) but without any animal-related products whatsoever, such as manure in the vineyards.

vegetal – A tasting note definitely open to interpretation. It suggests a smell or flavour reminiscent less of fruit (apple, pineapple, strawberry and the like) than of something leafy or even root-based. Some wines are evocative (to some tastes) of beetroot, cabbage or even unlikelier vegetable flavours – and these characteristics may add materially to the attraction of the wine.

vegetarian wine – Given that proper wine consists of nothing other than grape juice and the occasional innocent natural additive, it might seem facile to qualify it as a vegetable product. But most wines are 'fined' – clarified – with animal products. These include egg whites, isinglass from fish bladders and casein from milk. Gelatin, a beef by-product briefly banned by the UK government at the hysterical height of the BSE scare, is also used. Consumers who prefer to avoid contact, however remote, with these products, should look out for wines labelled suitable for vegetarians and/or vegans. The wines will have been fined with bentonite, an absorbent clay first found at Benton in the US state of Montana.

Verdejo – White grape of the Rueda region in NW Spain. It can make superbly perfumed crisp dry whites of truly distinctive character and has helped make Rueda one of the best white-wine sources of Europe. No relation to Verdelho.

Verdelho – Portuguese grape variety once mainly used for a medium-dry style of Madeira, also called Verdelho, but now rare. The vine is now prospering in Australia, where it can make well-balanced dry whites with fleeting richness and lemon-lime acidity.

Verdicchio – White grape variety of Italy best known in the DOC zone of Castelli dei Jesi in the Adriatic wine region of the Marches. Dry white wines once known for little more than their naff amphora-style bottles but now gaining a reputation for interesting, herbaceous flavours of recognisable character.

Vermentino – White grape variety principally of Italy, especially Sardinia. Makes florally-scented soft dry whites.

Vin Délimité de Qualité Supérieur – Usually abbreviated to VDQS, a French wine-quality designation between *appellation contrôlée* and *vin de pays*. To qualify, the wine has to be from approved grape varieties grown in a defined zone. This designation is gradually disappearing.

vin de liqueur – Sweet style of white wine mostly from the Pyrenean region of south-westernmost France, made by adding a little spirit to the new wine before it has fermented out, halting the fermentation and retaining sugar.

vin de pays – 'Country wine' of France. The French map is divided up into more than 100 *vin de pays* regions. Wine in bottles labelled as such must be from grapes grown in the nominated zone or département. Some vin de pays areas are huge: the Vin de Pays d'Oc (named after the Languedoc region) covers much of the Midi and Provence. Plenty of wines bearing this humble designation are of astoundingly high quality and certainly compete with New World counterparts for interest and value.

Vin de Pays Catalan – Zone of sub-Pyrenees region (Roussillon) of south-west France.

Vin de Pays de L'Hérault – Zone within Languedoc-Roussillon region of south-west France.

Vin de Pays des Coteaux du Luberon – Zone of Provence, France.

Vin de Pays des Côtes de Gascogne – Zone of 'Gascony' region in south-west France.

Vin de Pays de Vaucluse – Zone of southern Rhône Valley.

Vin de Pays d'Oc – Largest of the zones, encompasses much of the huge region of the Languedoc of south-west France. Many excellent wines are sold under this classification, particularly those made in appellation areas from grapes not permitted locally.

Vin de Pays du Gers – Zone of south-west France including Gascony. White wines principally from Ugni Blanc and Colombard grapes.

Vin de Pays du Jardin de la France – Zone of the Loire Valley.

vin de table – The humblest official classification of French wine. Neither the region, grape varieties nor vintage need be stated on the label. The wine might not even be French. Don't expect too much from this kind of 'table wine'.

vin doux – Sweet, mildly fortified wine mostly of France, usually labelled *vin doux naturel*. A little spirit is added during the winemaking process, halting the fermentation by killing the yeast before it has consumed all the sugars – thus the pronounced sweetness of the wine.

vin gris – Rosé wine from Provence. They call it *gris* ('grey') because it's halfway between red (the new black, you might say) and white.

Vinho de mesa – 'Table wine' of Portugal.

Vino da tavola – The humblest official classification of Italian wine. Much ordinary plonk bears this designation, but the bizarre quirks of Italy's wine laws dictate that some of that country's finest wines are also classed as mere *vino da tavola* (table wine). If an expensive Italian wine is labelled as such, it doesn't mean it will be a disappointment.

Vino de mesa – 'Table wine' of Spain. Usually very ordinary.

vintage – The grape harvest. The year displayed on bottle labels is the year of the harvest. Wines bearing no date have been blended from the harvests of two or more years.

Viognier – A grape variety once exclusive to the northern Rhône Valley in France where it makes a very chi-chi wine, Condrieu, usually costing £20-plus. Now, the Viognier is grown more widely, in North and South America as well as elsewhere in France, and occasionally produces soft, marrowy whites that echo the grand style of Condrieu itself.

Viura – White grape variety of Rioja, Spain. Also widely grown elsewhere in Spain under the name Macabeo. Wines have a blossomy aroma and are dry, but sometimes soft at the expense of acidity.

Vouvray – AC of the Loire Valley, France, known for still and sparkling dry white wines and sweet, still whites from late-harvested grapes. The wines, all from Chenin Blanc grapes, have a unique capacity for unctuous softness combined with lively freshness – an effect best portrayed in the *demi-sec* (slightly sweet) wines, which can be delicious and keenly priced. Unfashionable, but worth looking out for.

W

weight – In an ideal world the weight of a wine is determined by the ripeness of the grapes from which it has been made. In some cases the weight is determined merely by the quantity of sugar added during the production process. A good, genuine wine described as having weight is one in which there is plenty of alcohol and 'extract' – colour and flavour from the grapes. Wine enthusiasts judge weight by swirling the wine in the glass and then examining the 'legs' or 'tears' left clinging to the inside of the glass after the contents have subsided. Alcohol gives these runlets a dense, glycerine-like condition, and if they cling for a long time, the wine is deemed to have weight – a very good thing in all honestly made wines.

Winzergenossenschaft – One of the many very lengthy and peculiar words regularly found on labels of German wines. This means a winemaking co-operative. Many excellent German wines are made by these associations of growers.

woodsap – A subjective tasting note. Some wines have a fleeting bitterness, which is not a fault, but an interesting balancing factor amidst very ripe flavours. The effect somehow evokes woodsap.

X

Xarel-lo – One of the main grape varieties for *cava,* the sparkling wine of Spain.

Xinomavro – Black grape variety of Greece. It retains its acidity even in the very hot conditions that prevail in many Greek vineyards – where harvests tend to overripen and make cooked-tasting wines. Modern winemaking techniques are capable of making well-balanced wines from Xinomavro.

Y

Yecla – Town and DO wine region of eastern Spain, close to Alicante, making lots of interesting, strong-flavoured red and white wines, often at bargain prices.

yellow – White wines are not white at all, but various shades of yellow – or, more poetically, gold. Some white wines with opulent richness even have a flavour I cannot resist calling yellow – reminiscent of butter.

Z

Zefir – Hungarian white grape variety that can (on a good day) produce a spicy, dry wine rather like the Gewürztraminer of Alsace.

Zenit – Hungarian white grape variety. Produces dry wines.

Zinfandel – Black grape variety of California. Makes brambly reds, some of which can age very gracefully, and 'blush' whites – actually pink, because a little of the skin colour is allowed to leach into the must. The vine is also planted in Australia and South America. The Primitivo of southern Italy is said to be a related variety, but makes a very different kind of wine.

mercury (as compared to 90 ml in well-oxygenated human blood).

Next, the wines were opened. Further samples were taken after periods of two, four, six and 24 hours. For the first periods, the reading remained unaltered. Only after 24 hours had it increased significantly – to 61ml.

Meanwhile, the doctors tried pouring samples from another bottle of the wine into glasses and swirling it round. After only a couple of minutes, the reading reached 150.

Dr Agostoni was impressed. He returned to Milan and put his new-found wisdom to the test by inviting 35 friends to a party. He gave them all wine that had been swirled, and then wine that had been newly opened. Only two among the throng acknowledged no difference.

Then Dr A gave the guests a 'blind' tasting of swirled and unswirled wines. To his considerable satisfaction, all but one were able to tell the difference, and agreed the wine tasted significantly better with aeration.

Dr A passed these results on to his friend back in Idaho. The grateful Dr Charan was able to incorporate the information into a sideshow presentation at that year's meeting of the American Lung Association in Chicago. 'Just like blood,' Dr C told an enthralled audience of pulmonologists and thoracic surgeons, 'oxygenated wine is better than non-oxygenated wine.'

Glasses

Does it make any difference whether you drink your wine from a hand-blown crystal glass or a plastic cup? Do experiment! Conventional wisdom suggests that the ideal glass is clear, uncut, long-stemmed and with a tulip-shaped bowl large enough to hold a generous quantity when filled only halfway up. The idea is that you can hold the glass by its stalk rather than by its bowl. This gives an uninterrupted view of the colour, and prevents you smearing the bowl with your sticky fingers. By filling the glass only halfway up, you give the wine a chance to 'bloom', showing off its wonderful perfume. You can then intrude your nose into the air space within the glass, without getting it wet, to savour the bouquet. It's all harmless fun, really – and quite difficult to perform if the glass is an undersized Paris goblet filled, like a pub measure, to the brim.

Washing glasses

If your wine glasses are of any value to you, don't put them in the dishwasher. Over time, they'll craze from the heat of the water. And they will not emerge in the glitteringly pristine condition suggested by the pictures on some detergent packets. For genuinely perfect glasses that will stay that way, wash them in hot soapy water, rinse with clean, hot water and dry immediately with a glass cloth kept exclusively for this purpose. Sounds like fanaticism, but if you take your wine seriously, you'll see there is sense in it.

Keeping wine

How long can you keep an opened bottle of wine before it goes downhill? Not long. A re-corked bottle with just a glassful out of it should stay fresh until the day after, but if there is a lot of air inside the bottle, the wine will oxidise, turning progressively stale and sour. Wine 'saving' devices that allow you to withdraw the air from the bottle via a punctured, self-sealing rubber stopper are variably effective, but don't expect these to keep a wine fresh for more than a couple of re-openings. A crafty method of keeping a half-finished bottle is to decant it, via a funnel, into a clean half bottle and recork.

Storing it

Supermarket labels always seem to advise that 'this wine should be consumed within one year of purchase'. I think this is a wheeze to persuade customers to drink it up quickly and come back for more. Many of the more robust red wines are likely to stay in good condition for much more than one year, and plenty will actually improve with age. On the other hand, it is a sensible axiom that inexpensive dry white wines are better the younger they are. If you do intend to store wines for longer than a few weeks, do pay heed to the conventional wisdom that bottles are best stored in low, stable temperatures, preferably in the dark. Bottles closed with conventional corks should be laid on their side lest the corks dry out for lack of contact with the wine. But one of the notable advantages of the new closures now proliferating is that if your wine comes with a polymer 'cork' or a screwcap, you can safely store it upright.

──Wine and Food──

Wine is made to be drunk with food, but some wines go better with particular dishes than others. It is no coincidence that Italian wines, characterised by soft, cherry fruit and a clean, mouth-drying finish, go so well with the sticky delights of pasta.

But it's personal taste rather than national associations that should determine the choice of wine with food. And if you prefer a black-hearted Argentinian Malbec to a brambly Italian Barbera with your Bolognese, that's fine.

The conventions that have grown up around wine and food pairings do make some sense, just the same. I was thrilled to learn in the early days of my drinking career that sweet, dessert wines can go well with strong blue cheese. As I don't much like puddings, but love sweet wines, I was eager to test this match – and I'm here to tell you that it works very well indeed as the end-piece to a grand meal in which there is cheese as well as pud on offer.

Red wine and cheese are supposed to be a natural match, but I'm not so sure. Reds can taste awfully tinny with soft cheeses such as Brie and Camembert, and even worse with goats' cheese. A really extravagant, yellow Australian Chardonnay will make a better match. Hard cheeses such as Cheddar and the wonderful Old Amsterdam (top-of-the-market Gouda) are better with reds.

And then there's the delicate issue of fish. Red wine is supposed to be a no-no. This might well be true of grilled and wholly unadorned white fish, such as sole or a delicate dish of prawns, scallops or crab. But what about oven-roasted monkfish or a substantial winter-season fish pie? An edgy red will do very well indeed, and provide much comfort for those many among us who simply prefer to drink red wine with food, and white wine on its own.

It is very often the method by which dishes are prepared, rather than their core ingredients, that determines which wine will work best. To be didactic, I would always choose Beaujolais or summer-fruit-style reds such as those from Pinot Noir grapes to go with a simple roast chicken. But if the bird is cooked as coq au vin with a hefty wine sauce, I would plump for a much more assertive red.

Some sauces, it is alleged, will overwhelm all wines. Salsa and curry come to mind. I have carried out a number of experiments into this great issue of our time, in my capacity as consultant to a company that specialises in supplying wines to Asian restaurants. One discovery I have made is that forcefully fruity dry white wines with keen acidity can go very well indeed even with fairly incendiary dishes. Sauvignon Blanc with Madras? Give it a try!

I'm also convinced, however, that some red wines will stand up very well to a bit of heat. The marvellously robust Argentinian reds that get such frequent mentions in this book are good partners to Mexican chilli-hot recipes and salsa dishes. The dry, tannic edge to these wines provides a good counterpoint to the inflammatory spices in the food.

Some foods are supposedly impossible to match with wine. Eggs and chocolate are among the prime offenders. And yet, legendary cook Elizabeth David's best-selling autobiography was entitled *An Omelette and a Glass of Wine,* and the affiliation between chocolates and champagne is an unbreakable one. Taste is, after all, that most personally governed of all senses. If your choice is a boiled egg washed down with a glass of claret, who is to say otherwise?

———Index———